THE BACK HOME SERIES

Series Titles

Soul of the Outdoors
Dave Greschner

The Arc of the Escarpment
Robert Root

We Come from Good Stock
Kay Oakes Oring

Squatter
Yolanda DeLoach

Wildlifer
Neil F. Payne

From the Heart: The Story of Matrix
John Harmon

The Long Fields
Anne-Marie Oomen

Kick Out the Bottom
Erik Mortenson & Christopher Kramer

Wrong Tree: Adventures in Wildlife Biology
Jeff Wilson

At the Lake
Jim Landwehr

Body Talk
Takwa Gordon

The In-Between State
Martha Lundin

North Freedom
Carolyn Dallmann

Ohio Apertures
Robert Miltner

Praise for

Soul of the Outdoors

"In the tradition of Aldo Leopold and Annie Dillard, Dave Greschner employs both microscope and telescope in describing the world's minor miracles. For Greschner, no story is too small—not the ruby-throated hummingbird on its plastic perch or the bobolinks in the field. On the page, as in life, every bird and bug has meaning. Every bloom and blossom, too. Greschner writes of the world in the way I wish to see it: with knowledge, authenticity, and reverence most of all."

—B.J. Hollars
author of *Flock Together: A Love Affair with Extinct Birds*

"*Soul of the Outdoors* is part field guide, part almanac. Whether we join Dave Greschner while he's road hunting for firewood or cradling a saw whet owl on his snowshoe trail, we're right there with him every step of the way: from watching mulberry-tinged sunsets to discovering the first horned lark in the melt of winter."

—Patti See
author of *Here on Lake Hallie*

"Dave Greschner writes prose with lyrical poetry, helping the reader reconnect with the simple joys of childhood—times of playing outside until dark, exploring the natural world, letting that world be our first and best teacher. This is not just about remembering glory days of childhood. Through his writing, I connect with the natural world as a hectic and busy adult. This can provide the reader with moments of calm and grace."

—Timothy Goodwin
author of *Within These Woods*

SOUL
OF THE
OUTDOORS

reflections by

Dave Greschner

CORNERSTONE PRESS
UNIVERSITY OF WISCONSIN-STEVENS POINT

Cornerstone Press, Stevens Point, Wisconsin 54481
Copyright © 2023 Dave Greschner
www.uwsp.edu/cornerstone

Printed in the United States of America by
Point Print and Design Studio, Stevens Point, Wisconsin

Library of Congress Control Number: 2023950459
ISBN: 978-1-960329-24-0

Photographs by Dave Greschner

Cornerstone Press titles are produced in courses and internships offered by the Department of English at the University of Wisconsin–Stevens Point.

DIRECTOR & PUBLISHER   EXECUTIVE EDITORS
Dr. Ross K. Tangedal   Jeff Snowbarger, Freesia Mckee

EDITORIAL DIRECTOR   SENIOR EDITORS
Ellie Atkinson   Brett Hill, Grace Dahl

PRESS STAFF
Chloe Ciezynski, Carolyn Czerwinski, Kenzie Kierstyn, Sophie McPherson, Eva Nielsen, Natalie Reiter, Lauren Rudesill, Anthony Theil, Ava Willett

For Cathy,
and Mom and Dad

Contents

Life of Winter

January – February

It was quite daring. A 5-year-old could get hurt, or worse. Speed, poor lighting, waxed metal on iced snow, hard bumps and little margin for error. I faced it all with a face full of snow.

It was sliding. It was gripping steering handles resembling big wooden spoons while bouncing along belly-down on pine slats atop metal runners. All in the shadows of a dim amber yard light. The sliding hill started me down a straight slope in a rush. I met the driveway at an angle, leaned into a sharp right and leveled off as I coasted to the milk house. That is, if I avoided socking into the snowbank on the curve at the bottom of the hill.

I was a sledder, a slider, a snow rider, somewhat of an Olympic bobsledder. I squinted my eyes and set my jaw. It was winter. It was what a kid did.

Besides the sledding, there were also brief excursions to the pasture hill while carrying wide wooden skis that I was quite sure rode a boat from Norway. They could have, for my mother was a Scandinavian who fell in love with the German hired man. That man, my dad, flooded a snow-banked rink in the front yard so we could cut circles on ice. I built snow forts from which my dog and I guarded our home from imaginary enemies.

Though I was in winter, it was not always in me. It wasn't until after more than two decades of winters that I discovered the season's full magic, what I could do with it and what it could do with me.

By that odd age between kid and teenager, I had given up sliding, fort building, pasture hill skiing (which bore no resemblance to Olympic downhill racing) and ice skating (until some pond hockey years later on the flowage in town—a good excuse to get to town on Saturdays).

In those teenage years, what I liked most about winter was that it demanded little more of me than feeding and milking cows twice a day. That left a lot of time outside of school for reading, television, and playing in a basement rock band. College winters looked about the same, except for the social life on too many nights and weekends.

After college, I took my first job at a weekly newspaper. Winters were about to change. I was sent out on a story about a beaver trapper, a crusty cowboy of sorts who pulled no punches but whom I'd heard had thrown some. It was February of 1977, and the trapper was one of the originators and participants of the Yukon Jack World Championship Snowshoe Race, an endurance challenge with a long name for a long distance—83 miles.

I strapped on snowshoes to tag along for the story. Talk of the snowshoe race stuck with me more than the trapping story, to the point that I spent nearly a week's paycheck on two pairs of snowshoes. I started training, transfusing winter into my blood. It took. I snowshoed on crisp mornings with soft rosy sunrises, and on dreamy nights in the periphery of city lights.

Training runs stretched to 10 or 20 miles. I found I wouldn't freeze or get pneumonia. That was my mother's fear when she bundled me up in my childhood winters—I could barely move or see through the narrow slots for my eyes. The wind looked at me, gave up and moved on to some other little kid.

I did the snowshoe race, adapting to winter and its test of endurance. I had tamed the season with steady physical exertion and the right clothing. I added cross-country skiing for the racing and just to bushwhack around the snowy woods. Suddenly, I couldn't get enough of winter. I pursued rabbits and ruffed grouse, extending my hunting beyond the November deer, which had normally ended my woodland outings until spring. I even took a sled and chainsaw to the wintry woodlot to cut firewood.

The window on nature in winter had been opened. In the quiet cold and snow, I saw owls and foxes, animal tracks and vistas of leafless woodlands. Magical moments stopped me in my tracks—red cardinals aflame in popcorn-flake snow, mulberry-tinged sunsets, firewood smoke curling into the moonlit sky, geese shrouded in the rising steam of an open river on a sub-zero morning, and ruffed grouse erupting from a snow roost.

I inhaled the season, its air so fresh that I was invigorated in a way no summer's day could energize me. At the same time, it relaxed me. Wood heat and hot chocolate never felt so good as after a winter's day afield. That's still the case; I remain a user of winter, sometimes the best of times.

1

Stoking A Winter's Repose

The winter afternoon's repose is enhanced by its reflective calm. From the cushioned seat of a willow-frame loveseat, I stare at a turn-of-the-century cook stove. There's a dog on either side of me, their curled spines tracing the arcs of the willow branches cut, bent, formed and hammered together in the hills of northwest Arkansas a thousand miles away.

A braided rug soaks up the lingering moisture oozing from snow caught in the tread of my boots. There's soft afternoon light in the breezeway, flowing through the wide windows and blending with classic country music. The stove, the dogs, the rug, the willow, the music, and the calm oozing from a walk fill the crevices of my soul. So too does hope and wonder as a new year begins.

The soothing scene is repeated on as many days as possible. What I'm feeling here must also flow through the dogs after their walk. There are more comfortable nap nooks in the living room, but they, like me, choose the breezeway. Perhaps they like the view to the outdoors they just came in from, where rabbits and squirrels stir the hunter within them. More than anything, I think they feel my contentment, that satisfied state we all seek.

My gaze and thoughts veer back to the stove in front of me, wondering how many others sat near it on winter days. What were their thoughts, their hopes? Who fired the stove with wood, cooked on it, filled its water reservoir? How many children dried their mittens on its long, enamel-covered oven handle while they warmed their hands?

I stare at the all-capital letters, "QUICK MEAL STOVE CO. DIV. OF AMERICAN STOVE CO." Then I'm drawn to, "19-82 Serial 122, ST. LOUIS, USA." What train or truck did the 700-pound stove ride out of St. Louis? Who labored in the American Stove Co. factory to make a stove so durable that on a Thanksgiving Day a century later my wife cooked a turkey in it while I stoked the firebox? On such a rare call to duty, the stove remembers and delivers.

Someone cooked countless meals in and on this stove and undoubtedly listened to some of the same songs I'm hearing today on a radio station of vintage country music. Jimmy C. Newman is singing "Cry, Cry Darling." What strikes me is that the song now delivered via satellite was popular before this nation's first satellite was launched in

1958. Shortly after that, my parents were among the folks getting away from cooking and heating with wood in favor of propane gas—cheap at the time and requiring little labor.

This house was built in the early 1950s, when breezeways with windows and doors to the front and back yards routinely connected the house and garage. On New Year's Day the sun slants through the large windows facing the street to the west. Smoke flows from three other chimneys of close neighbors. We're back to burning wood. It's cheaper than oil but it's not easy, though my work is well spent.

The sun is low in the southwest and splintered by the bare branches of a small maple tree. It's going to be a cold night. The add-on wood stove in the basement is working to keep up. In a time past, the stove in front of me would be pitching in and cooking supper too.

I wonder what the new year will bring. Will it be as peaceful as this moment? If not, will I be as strong as the wide legs that hold up the stove's heavy grates and cast iron? Will we say goodbye to loved ones and friends, and hello to old friends, new acquaintances and newborns?

I suddenly realize I have a hand on each dog. I wish they wouldn't get another year older. I'd give up two of my years to keep them the same age for at least this year. To keep them beside me when the winter afternoon falls all around me. When the dogs, the stove, the music, and the willow are my comforts in a winter's reflective repose.

—Journals in January—

Opportunity

It was, at dawn's first light, just another winter morning. The birch tree looked the same as the day before, the familiar chickadees and nuthatches flitting about in its twigs and branches.

Bittersweet remained draped over the fence, its orange fruit breaking up the gray and white of winter. The pine boughs were dressed in a sprinkle of snow, just like yesterday. Sedum flowers again wore white caps.

Yes, there was a sameness on the surface. But I felt something anew on this first dawning of the new year. I could feel it on the clear morning as sunrise yawned across the horizon. What could be the newness?

Could it be that this morning begins a year of opportunity to fill my notebook with great horned owls hooting in the cold night, the first horned lark in the melt of winter, the discovery of a fawn on a spring hike, and of snow geese stringing across the cold blue of an autumn sky?

Will I find an agate? Watch a snapping turtle lay eggs on the gravel trail? See a coyote before it sees me? Watch grouselets follow the ruffed grouse hen? See a rare bird that sends me scrambling for my camera and field guide?

What's in your new year? A meteor streaking for several seconds in a black sky? A wildflower you've never noticed, waiting for you to identify? A jaw-dropping look at the Northern Lights? Maybe a cardinal feeding in the first burst of snow?

And after that snowfall, in the clearing night sky, will you step outside to look about in the light of the moon? And will it all be so fresh and entrancing in snow so pure that you feel like walking amongst it all? And will you keep walking, feeling nature's opportunities all about you?

Winter Numbers

Today's numbers further numb a frigid day in the throes of January. Negative numbers, mostly, as in minus 15°F with a minus 30°F wind chill. Three days in a row, with several inches of new snow thrown in.

So, I go looking for other numbers, those on the positive side or at least neutral. Today's sun sinks beyond the cold horizon of soft pinks and blues 24 minutes later than 30 days ago. Tomorrow morning, the sun will rise one minute earlier than today.

That chickadee at the feeder sports a half-inch coat of feathers. It weighs four-tenths of an ounce but will gain an additional 10% or more of its body weight today. Tonight, while perched, the chickadee will burn the fat of sunflower seeds and beef suet to stay warm, while also lowering its body temperature by 15 degrees to save shivering energy.

The leaping fisher of 30-some mph speed punctures the snow with tracks up to 16 feet apart as it hunts 10 square miles of range. Beneath 15 inches of ice, 32-inch northern pike cruise for 4-inch perch and bluegills. Ruffed grouse roosting in 12 inches of snow stay up to 35° warmer than when they perch in a pine tree.

Seven finches and a dozen pine siskins take turns at two feeders outside the kitchen window. Five juncos are below the backyard feeder. Three squirrels join them. Meanwhile, thousands of mosquitoes are buried beneath the snow, waiting for a day three months away.

Bear sows are giving birth to two or three 8-inch cubs. They weigh 4 to 5 ounces. Far above, a hawk sees light eight times better than I can, picking out a meadow mouse from 1,000 feet away. Hibernating chipmunks slash their heartbeats from 350 per minute to five.

I look at the calendar. There are 67 days until spring's vernal equinox.

Trails for Life

The first trails I followed were cow paths. They were pretty safe routes for a little tyke because they all led back to the farmyard. Safe at home.

I'd run along the narrow paths with a dog following, making up names for the paths that the cows slowly plodded along single file. The names originated from my latest childhood fascination with a television show—Route 66—or on a trip with my parents—Gunflint Trail.

I grew older and bolder in following trails, my interest peaked by their destinations as my explorations expanded. Cow paths turned into deer trails, and I'd follow logging roads, past and present. Eventually I found myself winding through the woodlands on cross-country skis. On ambitious days I'd ski for miles on groomed trails, sometimes snowmobile trails. I'd also stomp down my own snowshoe trails where few others ventured. Still do.

At a settling point in my life, new trails of a whole different plan and purpose came along. Trails forged in the backyard served a couple of four-legged boys—the puppies needed a route to stretch their legs and exhaust their energy in winter. The dogs' play path was triangular in shape, starting and ending at the foot of the deck (again, safe at home). After every snowfall I would shovel the 300 linear feet of dog trails and then smile at wagging dog tails above the banks.

A tossed ball would roll quickly down the slight incline, sending the boys hurtling into deep snow if they caught up to it too late. They didn't care. With gusto and white noses they'd find the ball in the powder and get back on track, one chasing the other to the triangle's next point.

Those trails are no longer; the boys are gone now. My energy goes back into the trails of exploration and recreation. I am grateful for the memories and hours of learning and laughing along those earlier paths. I am still learning and laughing on today's trails, all the while wondering but not worrying about the trails of the future. I look forward to them, wherever they take me, whatever they teach me, whenever they call me.

Somehow, life's trails always lead back home. Safe and warm at home.

2

Taking the Hills by Trail

When I first drove through the Blue Hills of northwest Wisconsin in the early 1980s, the trees elbowed in on the gravel roads as if intent on reclaiming their territory. They bowed from each side over the narrow road, creating a canopy of leafed beauty through the vast forestland. I found Bucks Lake Road by using a map. Perhaps there was a wooden marker or sign somewhere. I don't recall.

The Blue Hills cropping up in eastern Barron County and sprawling into Rusk County were as close to wilderness as I had experienced. Using Bucks Lake Road as my starting point, my old truck rumbled on washboard gravel as I snaked a bit further into the forest on each visit. I would stop to hunt ruffed grouse or to simply sit and be calmed by the quiet.

I noted my landmarks on plat books and gazetteers. I grew braver, hiking out further and further on trails that cut through the hundreds of acres of woods, being careful to remember the landscape where there was a choice of two paths. I was an explorer. It was my wilderness.

Decades later, the Blue Hills remain thousands of acres of forest, streams, flowages, lakes, swamps, hills and valleys. But the roads are wider, the trees cut back so far that their once leafy canopy is now only a memory. There are street signs, real estate signs, and warning signs telling all-terrain vehicle riders to stay on the road.

"Things are all changing, the world's rearranging a time that will soon be no more."—Dee Moeller, "Slow Movin' Outlaw"

Hoping that not all had changed, been rearranged, I went looking for the wooden signs marking road crossings of the Ice Age Trail, a footpath developed by those bent on preserving the area's natural features. I headed for Bolger's Road where it cuts west off Highway F near Murphy Flowage. After a mile, I saw the sign—yellow lettering on brown—marking the Ice Age Trail. I strapped on snowshoes and a backpack with a camera and headed south into the slanting sunlight of a mild January day.

I'd been on this portion of trail before, the previous July when bug spray was required and the vegetation so thick it choked the air. Ice Age Trail volunteers showed me a new footbridge through a wetland. In early fall, wolves attacked hunting dogs here. Now in the leafless winter woods hiding little, I had no fear of a surprise encounter. I headed for a point a mile and a half away.

The snowshoe tracks I followed were narrower than mine, but I easily widened the trail in the powdery snow. I hoped I was improving the path for the next person, which turned out to be me on the way back. Atop the hill overlooking Bolger Flowage and Hemlock Creek were two deer beds facing the winter sun, out of the biting north wind. I stopped, taking in the same panoramic view the deer had watched over. Then I caught a glimpse of two deer stepping slowly through the valley. They seemed oblivious to me before suddenly dashing away.

I stepped carefully along the switchbacks down the hill, reaching the creek that was open in spots and covered with ice formations in other places. Deer paths crossed the Ice Age Trail, the deer picking their way down small gullies to the water's edge. Along the path I followed were bobcat tracks.

After a bridge crossing that took 30 snowshoe strides, the trail climbed a hill high above the creek. There, I reached my planned turnaround spot after 55 minutes, with several pauses. I walked a bit further along Hemlock Creek and found the giant log a trail developer had shown me years ago. It was, as I expected, still there.

I pushed the pace on the way back, feeling sweat building under my wool shirt. I reached for my water bottle and squeezed it into my mouth. I suddenly and somewhat inexplicably felt blessed and thankful. I stared into the quiet vastness of the bare trees all around me, counting my gifts in silence.

It's easier to climb a steep hill on snowshoes than to descend it. In just over 3 minutes I had navigated the switchbacks easily, and though my breathing was labored, I also felt energized. My feet settled into my snowshoes, and my snowshoes into the trail. I had regained the snowshoe gait on this first outing of the winter.

Soon, *too* soon, through the bare branches I caught a glare off my pickup window. A breeze from the open road cooled me. I looked back and vowed to come back, hoping against "a time that will soon be no more."

—Journals in February—

Wind

As I veer off the tree-lined snowmobile trail and ply my snowshoes to a path through the open meadow, the wind finds my face. I lean through the trail's twists and turns in the night, but not in darkness. The ambient light from the nearby city joins a full moon above the clouds to light my serpentine way. I watch my snowshoes pounding into the furrow.

I come to a large field, its corn picked and the stubble barely poking above the snowpack. The wind is more noticeable here, catching all of me as I head west, the last row of corn as my guide. The clouds are racing eastward, the sky partially clearing, the wind shifting from southwest to northwest.

As I jog along, I think about the wind, how it dictates my direction and choice of clothes. I checked the wind, both direction and approximate speed, by the small windmill in the yard before I left.

Go into the wind first, I told myself, so it's at my back and pushing me home after I've worked up a sweat.

I also think about the wind changing directions and speed but never really changing at all. I can't see the wind, can't catch it, can't trace it. But I can feel it, right now, as I tug my collar a bit higher and my cap a bit lower. I hear wind songs in the night. On this night, it's "Against the Wind." *Still running against the wind.*

When I turn to head home the wind is my friend. However, if I think the wind is pushing me home I'm only half right for I'm also following the wind home. Poet Alan Alexander Milne wrote, "It's flying from somewhere as fast as it can, I couldn't keep up with it, not if I ran."

Saw-Whet

My first reaction was to scan the ground near the body, then the branches of the small white oak above it, and then again the ground, sweeping my eyes back and forth for evidence of a crime, signs of a struggle.

There were none. The only crime was that a saw-whet owl, one of the smallest owls, was dead, face down in the snow. Only its brownish back feathers showed, enough to catch my eye on a snowshoe hike.

I didn't know it was a saw-whet owl until I gently lifted its hand-sized body out of the soft snow. In another bittersweet moment in nature, I was thrilled at the find while mystified and saddened by the death.

How? Why? There were no marks on the owl, measuring 7 inches from its flat face to the tip of its tail feathers. It was folded neatly, as if it had died on its perch and fallen softly a few feet to the powder snow.

I held the bird in my hands, smoothing its rufous-streaked feathers. I studied its face, an outline of white forming a "V" on its forehead, reaching down to its beak and circling its eyes, the wide bands of white giving the appearance of a head too big for its body.

Its eyes didn't show the yellow of a saw-whet. They were nearly closed. Did the eyes cloud over when death came? Did death come because the same deep snow that softened its departing tumble also hid the owl's meals of mice? Was starvation the slayer?

Carefully and respectfully I nestled the rigid, soft-feathered body into my backpack; I knew a little budding naturalist who would want to see the owl. I had a small treasure, but I would rather that the owl had watched me walk past, its yellow eyes piercing my presence.

Moonlit Hike

Winter affords one, maybe two, opportunities to snowshoe or ski comfortably by the light of a full moon. The necessary trifecta is mild temperature, a mostly clear sky and, that big sphere, full or nearly so. In the last week of February it all came together under the Full Snow Moon.

So off I went, a couple of hours after sunset, the moon three hours into its night ride and already halfway up the eastern sky. The temperature had dipped below the freezing mark when I strapped on snowshoes and slapped them to the trail. I hoped to see animals moving in the moonlit meadow or the large field as I shuffled toward the narrow path in the forest. But the melting and freezing of previous days left a crust. *Crunch, crunch, crunch* spoke my snowshoes. I would not be sneaking up on anything.

 The full moon was behind me, my shadow waltzed in front of me. I crossed the field, the wide expanse allowing me to study the sky— Orion the Hunter and Sirius the Dog Star high in the south, the Big Dipper balancing on its handle in the northeast, and that big orb Full Snow, 225,000 miles away but seemingly riding on my shoulders.

The dark, jagged form of the hilly forest was a half-mile away. It wasn't that dark when I got there. My path was easily visible, a white ribbon tinged in blue, though always trailing into a dark curve. I'd reach the bend and see the next stretch of ribbon. I paused to listen for an owl, perhaps a coyote, but heard only the sifting of moonlight through the bare branches and pine boughs.

I headed for home, my shadow tagging behind to the jogging rhythm of my snowshoes. For a moment, it was nature's night song, on the wings of a Canada goose, in the gurgle of a creek, on the cadence of an owl's call. Sirius was my guide, high and straight ahead, with the moon towering to my left. Soft and peaceful was the night.

3

My Problem Is Firewood

It'll do me good to come clean. Admit my guilt, my failure, my shortcomings, my embarrassment. Face the music and deal with it. First off, however, let's preface the confession with the fact that it's been a long winter. A cold winter. A *long*, cold winter.

I've run out of firewood. There it is, my confession. Yes, I the woodsman, a persona I've groomed, ran out of wood before the woodchuck's day. The last dry chunks of 16-inch firewood were shoved into the stove on the last day of January. It was a cold night and the house was warm.

The house isn't warm anymore.

I'm ashamed of myself, and though I'm hearing others of woodsy ilk are in the same cold bind, that isn't making living with myself, or my chilly spouse, any easier.

"What? You had piles of firewood!" exclaimed a friend, who long ago fell for my Paul Bunyan act.

That's a friend. I haven't got to my wife yet. Well, I had a good amount of firewood but not piles and piles. I knew I was on the lean side. What I didn't know is that Mother Nature would turn to Arctic Nature starting in December and carrying on in January.

I started burning wood on October 16. Some nights I'd smirk in the comfy 70° while the natural gas furnace hibernated like a black bear. But on that last day in January, I came up the stairs, and there stood my wife in the kitchen. She was aware the firewood situation was getting dicey. She just didn't know I was getting down to my last shake.

"So are we out of wood now?" she asked, half in jest, expecting her saw-happy hubby to get defensive and say we had weeks and weeks to go. I did the right thing, well, the only thing I could because you can't lie about an empty wood rack.

"Yes," was my simple, honest answer.

The "Yes" hung in the air a time, curled like wood smoke in tense circles toward my wife's ears and settled somewhere in her incredulous mind.

"We are?"

Perhaps I should get defensive. Exhibit A: From a rural community sharing website there was a posting a week earlier that read, "Anyone have dry firewood? I, like others, misjudged how much firewood I would need this winter." Exhibit B: I really did take a vacation last May to cut firewood. It snowed. Heavy snow. In May.

To cut firewood in winter is to remind oneself of why you cut in spring and fall, and even in summer when the combination of sweat, chainsaw gas and bug spray can be pleasantly intoxicating. But when the cordless February dawned, I went to cut firewood, well aware there was too much snow to drive through the fields to the woods where there was also too much snow. But there were a couple of dead trees I'd noted on our land next to the road. This was their day.

Well, like a lot of things in life—my first-grade classroom comes to mind—the trees appeared bigger in my memory than they were when I pulled up next to them. But they were dry, and it was wood, so I went to cutting once I freed my legs from a ditch of snow deep enough to stall a giraffe. I cut rapidly, fearing someone would drive past and laugh, knowing a guy wouldn't cut firewood in February unless he was a loser who didn't cut firewood in September.

But I did cut in September. Honest. Oh, there were days of casual walks through antique shops and garage sales next to the big lake. But life is all about balance. And there were days—a lot of them I guess—in the tree stand, with a bow and arrow, while ironically surrounded by tons of potential firewood. But, again, balance.

After I cut up the two small trees, which will warm the house for perhaps two nights, I drove slowly along the town road, eyeing tree after tree. And then it suddenly hit me: I was road hunting for firewood! Right then I knew I had a problem. I had hit rock bottom. It whacked me over the head like a hunk of oak.

I will pay the natural gas bill the rest of the winter. But this won't happen again. I may be unbalanced, but I won't be cordless and cold.

Waiting for Spring

March — April

I have a black and white photo of a black dog asleep on a white sheet. The sheet has fallen from a clothesline in March, or perhaps April, decades ago. Though the snow has melted from the lawn, trees in the background are leafless on this cloudy day, warm and windy enough that my mother hung out washed bed sheets and pillowcases to dry.

The whites are fanning out to one side, telling me there is considerable breeze from the south. The wind was strong enough to loosen one sheet from its wooden clothespins. Ranger the dog has stumbled across this good fortune on the grass, just in time for naptime—a break from his spring explorations.

Ranger took advantage of what the day handed him. That is my approach in March and April, seemingly a 61-day dicey and icy bridge between winter and full-blown spring. The two months may offer us, without waiting for our approval or disapproval, more of winter, a little of spring, a feeling of summer, and then more of winter. They tease and please. They bury us in snow or boost us in spring fever.

I explore in March and April. I look for the white sheet on which to rest the hopes of spring. In childhood, I skipped along the pasture creek in search of pollywogs and frogs. I dug little ditches to drain the driveway of puddles so I could ride my bicycle. I raked acorns from the lawn where the snow had melted so I could bounce a ball off the house to simulate grounders on a ball field a month or more away.

Those were simple childhood rites of spring. Some years later I delved deeper into the season of awakening, inspired by Annie Dillard in her book, *Pilgrim at Tinker Creek*. Of spring, Dillard wrote, "I plan to control myself this year, to watch the progress of the season in a calm and orderly fashion. In spring I am prone to wretched excess."

March and April are not known for calm and order. We'd like to think that winter is over by the first day of March, or at least by the vernal equinox in the third week of March, and surely by the first day of April, all the while knowing it could be a fool's joke; one year I snowshoed on the first day of May. Of all the seasons, spring arrives more grudgingly and haltingly than others. It takes a step forward and then two backward, then a leaping stride forward on a day that feels like May, even summer. But it's not.

These months require patience, a stoic approach and a ready sweatshirt. And on those days when spring bursts through the budding branches, we are allowed wretched excess. We can count the robins on the lawn, see the emerging chipmunks, listen for frogs, watch winter running away down the hill. If we are fortunate, we will find the fallen white sheet on which to rest our winter weariness.

4

Morning in the Marsh

Good morning from the marsh. Two Canada geese, one to my left and another to my right, say "good morning" too, but I think it's to each other. I can't see them, but I can hear their throaty bark, sounding more like a "rrrrrrrrup" than a honk.

The geese are out there somewhere in the murky, stagnant swamp water, hidden by cattails, clumps of sedge grass, some saplings on spits of solid ground, and plenty of dead tree trunks and fallen branches. I'm hunkered low halfway down a steep bank that plunges from the railroad bed, the old grade that is now a trail that led me here.

I settle in for the morning marsh show in late March. The snow has melted, and ticks, I'm sure, have already pegged me. It's the price of admission for a seat on spring's bare ground padded with last fall's leaves.

I'm too low to see the geese, but I know who can see them. About two dozen great blue herons, migration arrivals in the past week, are perched in dead trees on the far side of the marsh. Their gray feathers have taken on an amber hue from the rising sun, which for now is kissing only the treetops while a plump moon falls in the background.

Two wood ducks jump from a channel of water only 30 feet away. We have startled each other. I look around for an old tree trunk that may provide their nesting hole. The channel is separated from the swamp by a beaver dam, which I suspect is partially responsible for the high water in the swamp.

There is suddenly a commotion at one of the heron nests. I can clearly see about a dozen nests, but there are more behind the obvious ones a hundred yards across the swamp. The nests are arrangements of sticks in the crotches of dead branches high in bare trees. Some trees have two nests, two stories as it would be, the supporting branches less than 10 feet apart. None of the nests appear able to withstand a spring thunderstorm. But they do.

I don't know what ignited the ruckus. The herons are mating, and it appears that a mating attempt in one nest drew the attention of nearby birds, until four birds are flailing above that nest. There are wide wings, long necks and gangly legs everywhere, all somewhat synchronized to squawking disagreements and accusations, like drunks shouting at each other with hoarse voices.

And then it's over in seconds. I look down to see a tiny spider working its way across my notebook. And there's a wood tick clinging to the paper's edge. I flick them away, while in the brush to my left a ruffed grouse picks up the drumming beat of wings.

The herons have decided to get on with what matters. It's a workday. They are repairing nests in the colony. Every few minutes a heron starts flapping its wings and lifts off rather laboriously, pumping its 6-foot wingspan until it gains flying speed—up to 23 miles per hour—before it glides out of sight above the hardwoods to the north.

The bird reappears in minutes with a single stick in its beak, announcing its return with a *"roh, roh, roh"* while thrusting its feet forward for landing. Its wings spread wide to slow the approach. Another heron's head pokes out of the tangle of sticks and stretches its long neck to meet the arriving bird's beak. The stick is exchanged deftly and slowly, as if it's a long-stemmed rose from one lover to another.

The nest bird meticulously works the stick into place while the carry bird watches. Within a minute, the stick is where it needs to be and the whole process starts over again. This is happening at every nest, though not constantly. Sometimes the herons sit quite still, like old men with white hair in gray overcoats, watching and waiting. Then the herons preen, touch each other's beaks, and, at times, turn their heads to watch a bald eagle cruise above the swamp.

I watch the eagle too. Then I bring my gaze to eye level to see tree swallows perched on small dead trees in front of me, and a dozen red-winged blackbirds in the cattails. A hawk wings over without malice, but the blackbirds can't help but give chase just the same. A pileated woodpecker rises and falls, disappearing with a laughing taunt behind the deep red of maple tree buds.

The geese have been calling without pause as they slowly navigate around swamp obstacles and meet up in the middle. There's a loud splashing of water not far in front of me, but out of sight behind grasses and sticks. I don't think they're fighting—quite the opposite.

This is the noisiest solitude I know. Two hours have passed quickly during this show of many plots and characters. There's no ending in sight. I think of the first line of an Emily Dickinson poem by the same name, "Sweet is the swamp with its secrets."

—Journals in March—

Order of Assurance

From atop a hill my vantage point of the lake gives me cause to pause. As does the silence. I don't know which drew me here the most, but now I'm thinking it is something more than the landscape and lack of noise.

As I look down on the lake, still covered in ice and snow, I understand that nature has order, and that feeds my reflective mood. I know the ice will melt, then the migrant ducks will arrive, and so too will the songbirds all along the greening shore.

There will be the sequence, structure and succession of spring, the same as last year but somehow all new again, all in nature's amazing timing and excess.

Hounded and chased by bad news, I took to the outdoors. There is always nature, the outdoors, offering a diversion from worries and the hectic pace we thrust on ourselves. Nature is the tonic, a healthy haven for body and soul, where we clear our heads and breathe fresh air. I touch the maple tree trunk with its sweet sap oozing out, urged on by March's afternoon sun which also urged me to come here. And "here" hasn't failed me.

Henry David Thoreau wrote in the 19th century, "There are moments when all anxiety and stated toil are becalmed in the infinite leisure and repose of nature." Frank Lloyd Wright observed a century later, "Study nature, love nature, stay close to nature. It will never fail you."

We all can't walk the woods and shorelines, but we all can let nature take over our thoughts for a time, move the troubled horizon for a moment or more, perhaps simply by watching a bird feeder, a sunrise, or the melting ice in the order of spring's reveal.

Slowly, yet surely, nature is consistent in its tranquility, peace and pace. Worries becalmed.

Surrender to Vernal

Winter is running down the hillside, worming its way into small streams that will only be a trickle, if that, in summer. Winter is chased across the sloping meadow, into the corn-field, then to the roadside where it races for a grated hole in the curb.

What a trip. From a snowflake in November, free-falling to this hillside to spend the winter nestled with millions of other snowflakes atop the decaying leaves. The snowpack now feels the tilt of the earth and a bright nuclear fusion power 92 million miles away. Gravity won't let this collection of snowflakes reverse course; the snowpack surrenders to melting and runs downhill.

Some transformed snowflakes are bound for bodies of water they passed over in their freefall months ago. Others will give up the race, settle into the field to help sprout whatever seed they're given to nourish in spring planting.

I walk over the remaining snow where it clings stubbornly in spits and patches beneath the thick cover of prickly ash, in the murky light beneath the pines, and on the north side of hills where the sun has been a stranger for months. It's a little bit winter and a whole lot of spring, cool in the shade and warm in the sun. There are fresh tracks of deer and new scat of bears. Divots where squirrels dug for acorns are revealed among dead leaves now reappearing but remaining compacted from winter's burden of snow.

The snow knows it is time to go. There are rivers to rise and crops to grow. Winter is running down the hillside, surrendering in front of my eyes.

Tom Turkey

Knowing I'm not invited, I attempt to stay on the edges, blend in where I can and always, always, be quiet. I am the interloper on a morning in early spring as I follow a soft and sometimes muddy path up and down through the woodlands and meadows.

I crest a hill where the corner of a field rises to meet the fence line and woods. And there is a turkey, a lone stalker of companionship in dawn's murky light.

The tom didn't see me moving. I freeze, half my body in the turkey's line of sight if he looks my way and deciphers what he's looking at. Incredibly, he struts closer and closer, leaving only a narrow strip of sparse, leafless brush and a retiring fence between us. Then the turkey stops, about 20 feet away.

The tom didn't stop because he saw me. No, instead he has apparently found the perfect spot to gobble. The head juts forward and a long beard—perhaps 10 inches—dangles from the outstretched neck. There's one gobble, a pause, another gobble.

I watch this repeated for several minutes. I have no camera, though the slightest movement to take a photo would send the gobbler scrambling. Choosing to change the narrative and relieve my frozen position, I take a few steps forward. The bird runs. So I run, the two of us racing parallel on either side of the fence line.

The turkey gains ground on me and then cuts in front of me, crossing my path well ahead and disappearing into the woods. I catch my breath while furrowing into memory a vision of the last few minutes.

Five minutes later I roust more than a half a dozen turkeys from their pine tree roosts. They awkwardly gain clearance, wings audibly laboring to lift 20 pounds or more on their escape. The turkeys flush in singles and pairs. I try to see just one before it flies, but I can't. They are camouflaged and wary. I am in the open and scary.

It's a spring morning for turkeys. Strutting, gobbling, roosting, flushing, flying. I sweep through the valley and turn for home. The turkeys are already home.

5

Last Waltz on Ice

As I walked gingerly across the lake, its deteriorating ice granulated like molasses cookies, a hint of a coolness rode the southerly wind. It was as if someone opened a refrigerator door on a warm afternoon. The cooler air, as near as I could figure, came from the wind passing over a long stretch of lake, picking up the chill of the ice. But for the most part the air above the lake was warm, surpassing 80°F on this summery day in April.

The shoreline was rimmed with water as ice pulled away. In the middle of the lake, however, ice was a foot thick in the fishing hole I was staring down on what would be the last day of ice fishing. I am the least likely person to be out on the last day. I can take or leave ice fishing. Walking on dicey ice? I normally always leave that alone.

So why was I on the ice, casting my fate to the spring melt? Was I simply following my friend and believing him that the ice was safe? Was I trying to show that I was brave enough to do something different? And maybe catch supper?

I looked around and figured there was safety in numbers. Quite a few other folks were fishing. A snowmobile and four-wheeler motored past as my friend scoffed at the idea of weak ice. He said a guy we know, who weighs a good feed sack more than I do, was fishing there that morning.

Wearing only a T-shirt, blue jeans and sneakers, I walked away from land, stepping along the dock over a spit of open water to reach the ice. In the breeze, I thought I heard my mother's voice, "If your friend jumped off the bridge, would you jump too?"

The fish were biting like wild, but most of them could turn circles in a shot glass. We pulled up a few keepers. An older fisherman, who looked as if he had spent the winter on the ice, wasn't doing any better. Presuming his seniority made him wiser in these matters, I felt better that he was also on the ice. The April ice.

The oldtimer yanked up a small bluegill and muttered something about its size, twisted it off the hook and dropped it back down the hole. "You can't get past the little ones to the big ones," he said, adding that it had been like that most of the season. But he hadn't given up nor seemed too concerned about anything. He sat there in bib overalls on the required five-gallon pail, patiently watching his line, hoping to get a wax worm into a big bluegill's mouth.

In stark contrast, some younger guys who were sampling beer and schnapps not far away jabbed each other with profanity-laced fishing boasts. They weren't catching fryers either, but the biggest fish of the day would win a bet.

Ducks winging overhead proclaimed there was open water nearby. Probably pretty close. Perhaps in the bays of this lake. I looked to where I had left the truck on the shoreline. It now seemed far away. I kind of wished I were in the truck, rolling through the greening countryside, listening to a baseball game.

The bobber went down and I yanked the rod up. Another small one. For entertainment I laid the fish about a foot from the hole and watched it flip itself back to open water, do a circle and shoot downward.

Clouds started to build in the west; the afternoon grew gray and cool. Not wishing to break through the ice, especially in the dark, I bid good-bye to my fishing partner and headed for shore. Walking alone, I was suddenly scared. I hesitated when I saw dark spots and cracks in the ice, carefully tip-toeing around them.

The ice had taken on a more ominous appearance in the past few hours. Every step closer to land was precious. I thought about running, but then thought again. If I fell I might crash heavily to the ice and through it. The shoreline grew larger, the anglers behind me smaller. I reached the dock and skipped onto shore, feeling safe. Though I was performing only for myself, I acted like I was never scared. I had that smug feeling of getting in and out of the cookie jar unscathed.

The next day, I was told, ice had surrendered substantially, to at least 30 feet from the dock. No one was on the lake, they said. I had been out on the last day of pulling fish through round holes in the ice. Nothing I would recommend. Nothing I would do again.

—Journals in April—

Comfort

What is the comfort in the return to something familiar? Why does it feel that good to return to what we know, what we like, what is comfortable? Perhaps we are returning in spirit or flesh or both, to where we were happiest.

Spring is a return, a happy return, to what we like, what we know will be pleasant. We remember it as being exciting, with creeks and frogs, kites and balls, and explorations along trails abandoned since fall.

And perhaps it explains the anticipation and excitement in another return, that of songbirds once again choosing our field, our yard, our trees to start anew with nests and chicks and the whole propagation of the species.

The return of birds now dominates the conversation of the folks I hang around. A friend calls daily to report new sightings—a loon, killdeer, grackles and bluebirds. The sightings turn into friendly competition, as in who sees what first.

But through it all, there's comfort in the next sighting, no matter by whom, for it's another affirmation of migration. For what if the birds didn't return?

Amid the comfort, however, there's a bit of irritation, a sticker in the sock, for birds not easily identified suddenly appear and flit away. It drives me crazy.

I came around a corner on a woodland trail the other day, and half a dozen rust-colored birds danced away through the leafless branches. A hue of rust on a body 6 to 8 inches long is all I could gather. Veery? Brown thrush? Something other?

No matter what, they had returned. I found comfort in that.

Cottontail Gang

There's trouble brewing in the neighborhood. This morning the trouble had 16 legs and was beneath the front yard bird feeder.

Then trouble fled, four legs at a time carrying furry gray bodies across the top of crusted snow. Trouble gathered in a loose unit beneath the pine tree, assessed the situation, and then scrambled in synchronized frenzy toward the street.

Trouble took a hard right and ran down the plowed roadway. Four young rabbits were running away as would four kids escaping an apple raid. They blended into one faraway blur as they rounded the corner.

At least it was a sign of spring. But, I know the rabbits may present problems down the line, more so for those neighbors who have gardens than for me with my modest plot of potato plants in plastic pails.

And, I should admit, rabbits sneaking into the fenced-in backyard—the young ones can slither through the gate—is less of a problem now than when I had young dogs. My four-legged boys insisted on chasing the frightened cottontails until both pursued and pursuers nearly collapsed of exhaustion.

Exhaustion, that is, if the rabbit was lucky. One day my dogs sent a rabbit into the fence, its head poking through an opening as my persistent poodles nipped at its haunches. There was no turning back for anyone, literally or figuratively.

I from one side of the fence and the big neighbor dog from the other ran to the site of calamity for a look. What happened next is unforgettable and unforgivable, I guess on all three dogs' accounts. Let's just say the rabbit lost its head in a three-dog fright.

The canines in that gruesome scene have all passed on now. And the rabbits don't bother me much anymore. But four of them in a spring gang? There will be trouble somewhere in the neighborhood come summer.

Bluebirds

There is something quite satisfying in being stirred by the simple sight of the first bluebird of spring. This bird wearing the blue sky on its back has returned from a thousand miles away to spend spring and summer in a nesting box I built specifically for it. It sends a shiver through me on a warm day in April.

And so I hoped, as I turned onto the town road that passes the fields of our family farm, that maybe this day, this 11th day of April, would be the day.

It was, and it was dou-ble-special as my mother was with me. If I had a nickel for every time she told me that bluebirds were her favorite bird, well, I'd have a lot of nickels. Maybe enough for a bluebird coin bank to go along with mom's bluebird salt and pepper shakers.

Over the past few years I've made bluebird boxes in winter and placed them along the hayfield in March. And then I wait for my birds of blue to return to the fields where the grasses of hay aren't cut until late June. That means ground-nesting bobolinks have a safe haven to hatch chicks, while bluebirds and tree swallows wing above the swaying grasses, feeding on insects. They all get along.

As we approached the bluebird house on the hill, I saw the silhouette of a bird atop the slightly-sloped barnboard roof. The bluebirds were back. Mother Nature had smiled on me and my mother, who was also smiling. A few days shy of her 92nd birthday, she was thrilled with the present of spring wrapped in blue feathers.

6

Cold and Wet, and Yet, Birdy

It's a morning in late April, so birding should be bursting with songbirds returning, or passing through to points farther north. At the same time, overwintering birds are chirping territorial and nesting songs of spring.

But it's 39°F with persistent spits of rain riding a biting east wind. I tug a little more at the zipper of my winter coat and look out the truck window for my guide, hoping she shows, understanding if she doesn't.

Laura Sandstrom shows up. I pretty well knew she would. The bird woman, as I call her, isn't going to miss an opportunity to share the trail and her observations with another bird enthusiast. As we greet each other, I notice the rain has stopped for a moment, or perhaps for Laura.

We step onto the Wild Rivers Trail. I begin peppering Laura with questions about bird watching, which I am about to find is a lot about bird listening. She begins looking for any movement in the brush along the trail. But mostly she's listening, which I'm a little slow to pick up on.

I suddenly realize I'm like the little kid you take deer hunting. The kid who won't shut up until you make it known no deer will be seen until there is quiet. I figure this out as Laura politely, softly answers my questions as she studies the brush with both eyes and ears.

"White-breasted nuthatch," she says, pointing off the trail in the direction of a nasal-sounding "*yank, yank, yank.*"

Laura has been birding for 20 years, ever since her daughter returned from a college biology trip to Costa Rica and shared her bird watching adventures with her mother. "There was an awakening of something inside me I didn't know I had," recalls Laura.

Laura keeps an annual bird journal along with a "birding lifebook." That lifebook, for example, notes 28 different species of warblers, all seen by Laura in her local outings.

The first bird we spot on this gray day is a wild turkey, not necessarily what we came to see but welcome nonetheless as it crosses the trail. That might be it for this day, so I thought. Just past a short footbridge, which carries the trail across a small creek, there is a large swampy pond stretching between the trail and a heron rookery on the far side. "This is a good spot. I can stand still here for 20 minutes," says Laura.

We count up to a dozen herons on nests as I take photos with cold fingers. Laura remains intent on the scene in front of us, lifting her binoculars to her eyes now and then to survey the wetland below. "There's something down in there," she says softly, then quickly adding, "Chickadee and female red-winged blackbird."

Laura then notices a Canada goose standing motionless on the side of the swamp. She continues to glass the water, clumps of grass and dry cattails. I see movement in the water next to the goose. Laura swings her binoculars to where I point.

"Oh, very good," she says while I wonder what I've spotted. She notes aloud the markings on four ducks. "Teal?" she asks herself while reaching into her pocket for one of two field guides she's carrying.

"Not green teal. What's the other teal? Yes, blue teal. That's it," Laura says, noting a distinguishing crescent mark by the ducks' eyes.

There's more movement closer to us, in the sticks and weeds reaching above the water surface. Laura is working the glasses again when she exclaims, "Yellow-rumped warbler!" It's her first warbler sighting this spring, and it raises some excitement even if the veteran birder knows the yellow-rumped warbler and all the other warblers will arrive in time.

A ruby-crowned kinglet lands no more than 10 feet in front of us, giving Laura the perfect opportunity to explain that bird watching is often about standing still and letting the birds come to you.

I thought the morning would be birdless. I thought wrong. In 30 minutes we've seen turkey, teal, warbler, phoebe and kinglet, along with the usual fare of robins, chickadees, crows and blackbirds.

As we backtrack to our vehicles, Laura seems satisfied with this outing in April. She's also brimming with anticipation. "Look out for May. There will be a bird explosion," Laura predicts, just as cold rain picks up again.

Puppies, Campers, and Hayfields

May – June

It's May, rushing toward Memorial Day, with June's greenness and solstice in the wings, ready to deliver what is so rare as a day in early summer. It's finally spring with all its newness and nesting. I want to stand and stare, and explore, find the first trillium, the first yellow-rumped warbler, and perhaps pollywog eggs if I want to return to my childhood.

Frogs and baseball pretty much filled my May days back then. I had not yet come to appreciate and trace nature's spring revival. I only waited for the creek to run and frogs to magically appear from what I would later learn was a frozen winter existence in the stream bottom's mud.

I hoped for a dry spring to bounce a rubber ball off the milk house wall onto a dirt driveway. Grounders, I was always fielding grounders. I also played ball on the south side of the house, that is, after picking up last fall's acorn crop. Rubber balls took bad bounces on acorns, though I suppose that was good grounders practice too.

That those days were so filled with only two activities, outside of the achy last month of school, seems somewhat implausible compared to my spring outdoor excesses now.

I keep a lookout for migrating songbirds, awakening chipmunks, nesting ruffed grouse, butterflies, and bear cubs. I watch for crappies to come in shallow to spawn, look for agates exposed in the creeks after the rush of snowmelt, or pick wildflowers for someone on May Day. Or any day in May.

Some days I just walk the land to watch it green. To watch the days grow long and feel the warmth stay around. To know that summer is now more than a hope.

On the summer solstice I hope to be at the campfire, hope to be as reluctant as the sun to give up the day, at the same time eager to welcome the cool and starry night. What was a dream in January is now here. Summer.

7

Puppies' First Spring

Acouple of little guys came into our life last November, and life hasn't been the same since. They are two inquisitive hairy faces watching and following my every move. They want my attention, encouragement, approval, and my socks.

They are tireless and I am tired. They cost a lot of money, and every bill is times two. They play, bark and fight during the evening news. They run faster than me on the trail. They sleep in seven mornings a week.

They want to be fed constantly and have discovered popcorn. My bowl goes down faster. They throw up now and then, here and there. It takes more time to work on outdoor projects as I unplug power tools when not in use lest the puppies bite into the hot cord. I unplug. They carry the unplugged cord across the lawn.

They sometimes get up at 3:30 in the morning for a potty run outside, or just a drink of water. I sleep light and less.

And I love every minute of it.

When we took on the bichon/poodle puppies, they were eight weeks old, my wife and I midlife, as in crisis perhaps. That may have been the push for the first dogs ever in our house. If there was a crisis, the "boys" have become the cure for it. Sort of empty nest syndrome in reverse.

We picked out two—half-brothers— from two litters. The woman brought out a third puppy, just as cute, but we stopped at two. This wasn't a full-blown midlife crisis. We had some sense.

Smokey had black hair that would turn silvery gray as he got older, thus the name I gave him. Max had curly gray hair. They were too cute—all puppies are—and there was joy in our home, at least for a couple of days until reality and anxiety hit. "What did we do?"

We wondered if the pups would ever get this thing called house-trained. Would they ever be trusted beyond the breezeway's floor of newspapers? Would my wife and I ever have freedom again?

But by spring the eight-week-old puppies were eight-month-old puppies, house-trained and with rights to the entire house. It took some doing, including many winter nights taking the dogs outside under the watch of Sirius the Dog Star and a hooting great horned owl. The boys lifted their cold paws and stared at me, and I wondered how I could tell them the cold and snow would pass.

I tried, but Smokey and Max would only cock their heads inquisitively as if to ask, "What is spring?" And now they know. Spring is a big backyard with no shoveled trails through the snow. It's last fall's leaves to roll in and this spring's new earth to dig in. It's grackles and robins they can't catch, and the cooing of mourning doves to perk up their ears.

Spring is the first bumblebee to vibrate on their noses, kids to bark at in the park on the other side of the fence, a lawn mower to chase, and a butterfly too. It's a clear creek to jump in and drink from (What? No dish?). It's waiting for a hamburger from the grill.

Sometimes, exhausted from their explorations and ball playing, it's simply lying on your side in the new grass, in the warm sun, looking at your half-brother and taking a little paw-punch at him once in a while.

Now, do I tell them that winter will come again?

—Journals in May—

Chipmunk

Chippy makes its home in the yard shed, the rock garden or the woodpile, depending on the time of day. Watching over three homes, not to mention foraging for meals, makes for a busy life for Chippy, and my watchful dogs.

Chippy is either quite confident of his or her speed or has never had a close encounter with a canine. It dashes past in broad daylight with hairy faces nearby. One of my dogs caught a chipmunk years ago after a cat-like stakeout near the woodpile. The current Chippy is apparently not related to the deceased Chippy.

The striped rodent with puffy cheek pouches provides a pastime for the dogs while posing no real threat to its (ours) various properties, including the garage, where we share time and space. As spring greens toward summer there are pests aplenty. Chippy is not one of them. High-strung and everywhere at once, yes, but not a pest.

My wife asked how many more critter battles must we fight as I showed her the raised trails of moles on the lawn. First moles in years, and as I ponder the problem, a mosquito bites me. And I think I feel a tick.

Most of spring is consumed with dissuading yellow-bellied sapsuckers from turning my mountain ash tree into a cribbage board. They've killed one tree. I won't let them kill another.

A few steps away, a ground bee disappears into a hole in the flower garden. I contemplate the solution to this while Chippy scurries past with two dogs in tow.

Birdbaths

There was rain in the overnight forecast. I could have just let the birdbaths stay dry for the rest of the afternoon. They were bone dry, beckoning for my attention as I sat on the deck with a cup of coffee.

For a day in late May there was little activity in the yard, usually teeming with songbirds' spring frenzy of singing, nesting, feeding, bathing, and preening. Could I change

 the scene? I put down my coffee cup, turned on the hose faucet and filled both bird-baths, which double as drinking fountains for the feathered. Oh, yeah, the furred too.

I turned the faucet off, put the hose away and returned to my coffee. Within two minutes, I kid you not, the backyard came alive. A chipmunk led off, jumping on the concrete bath shaped like a giant leaf and resting near the ground on three rocks.

After sips of water, the chipmunk left and was immediately replaced by a robin, which had been waiting for its bath. Water spraying from its wings told me so.

I looked to the other concrete birdbath, this one on a stand next to the birch tree trunk. A phoebe landed and sipped. It left as a goldfinch arrived, joined by a cedar waxwing. They got along but neither let down its guard.

The goldfinch flew away, signaling a second waxwing to join its mate in happy hour. Suddenly they both lifted off and landed in the mountain ash tree to shake off water. Then a robin came to the birdbath, and this messiest of birdbath users stirred the water.

Later came a cardinal and catbird. And more finches, and a chickadee or two. Then the squirrels got thirsty. To think, all this because I put my coffee down for a few minutes and turned on the water.

By the way, it didn't rain that night.

Nesting Grouse

I've come nose to beak with a few ruffed grouse but never for the surprise staredown like the one in the maple woods this spring. I had returned to where I inadvertently flushed a grouse off her nest of a dozen eggs a week earlier.

The simple ground nest of a bowl of leaves was at the base of the maple tree, with greening forest understory and blooming trilliums draping over it. I nearly stepped on it before the grouse hen reluctantly and, I hoped, temporarily abandoned incubation.

Thrilled at the discovery but regretting my interruption, I quickly counted 11 buff-colored eggs and was on my way in the opposite direction of the hen's flight.

I came back with a camera a week later. I slowly and stealthily approached the nest side of the tree, holding my camera ready for the first unobstructed view of the grouse.

I saw her through the leaves, hunkered down in the nest. I stopped and lifted the camera to my eye.

She didn't flush, didn't stretch her neck as the wary hunted grouse of autumn do before flushing. This time this hen was sticking to her eggs, hoping I wouldn't come closer. I didn't.

From 20 feet away I took what I could get. The camera stared at the bird, the bird stared back. I took a couple of photos and then turned on the flash, hoping to light the shaded scene. Two flash photos. The bird didn't flinch.

I didn't push my luck. Twice I have been chased by ruffed grouse, but that wasn't my concern here; I didn't want to disrupt the sitting hen again. In the quiet spring woods, the hen stayed on the eggs as if she knew my intentions. I was gone in a matter of a minute, leaving behind a wish for a hatch below the canopy of spring green.

8

Hitch Up the Camper

It was 1990 and Lake Ouachita, give or take a year or lake. No, not a lake. Pretty sure I'm right on that, having got the spelling down if not the pronunciation. It's hard to forget 40,000 acres of sprawling water in west central Arkansas, its fingers and claws reaching out from the main reservoir, appearing on the map as a squished squid.

It was at a campground, retired folks sitting around tables and campfires outside their home-away-from-home on wheels. My wife's uncle Dave was told noon lunch was ready, this after a big breakfast only a few hours ago and before the evening meal would fill the picnic table and those around it.

Uncle Dave nodded toward the fifth-wheel camper and drew upon his cattle dealing days to observe, "These things ain't nothing but fattening pens."

That night, as flames teased each other in the fire pit, a local who had become friends of my wife's parents and aunt and uncle, took a long draw on his pipe upon hearing his wife wanted to run into Hot Springs 40 miles away the next day to get something at Walmart.

"When I die …" he drawled, then a long pause for effect followed by words pulled slowly and oh so smoothly from the dancing darkness, "…just scatter my ashes on the Walmart parking lot. That way my wife can visit me every day."

That's what I remember from driving south, sans camper, to visit the "old folks" who were camping snowbirds in snow-less Arkansas. I remember that and sunrises and sunsets on Lake Ouachita, grilled burgers and steaks, the southern breeze in the pines, the smell and warmth of campfire smoke as the day cooled off, and short drives to little mountain and lake towns called Mount Ida, Hurricane Grove, Washita, Story, and Fannie.

I had nothing to do with hitching and unhitching camp-ers, backing them up, pulling forward, backing up again, pulling forward, over and over, leveling, blocking, and run-ning electrical cords, water hoses, and sewer drains. It was all taken care of by my father-in-law, a cattle hauler who felt at home behind the wheel, on the road, pulling some-thing, anything.

I wondered if that was my future. Not the cattle hauler part, but the fifth-wheel camper deal. Well, the future is here. My wife and I are new owners of a fifth-wheel. It's only 26 feet long. I say "only" because my father-in-law would have laughed at the short rig. He wasn't happy unless he was pulling well over 30 feet of camper, all the better with a boat behind the camper. That towing length got him stopped once or twice. He was proud of it.

Not me. I'm fine with 26 feet, would have been good with 16 feet, but there's the matter of marital bliss at the campground. Room for separation prevents filing for separation.

I am not a hauler, so even pulling out of the camper/car dealership lot got my eyes bugged out and knuckles white on the steering wheel, wondering how many vehicles I would wipe out. I was sure I would hit another camper at the least. But I made it out of the lot unscathed, only to face the decision of a roundabout or pulling onto the freeway ramp. I took the ramp. Why push my luck?

I found a big, empty lot to practice backing up my new 26-foot home. There was, however, a semi-truck driver at the far end of the parking lot, eating lunch and watching. Geez.

I'm sure the neighbors back home were waiting for a good show and laugh, but I got the basics down in the parking lot. Without hitting the semi. And then I headed for our street. My wife scrambled out of the truck and shouted, "I'll make sure you don't hit the mailbox!" I was 30 feet away from the mailbox. She wasn't exactly building up my confidence.

It went well. And now there it sits, like a doll house on steroids. I'm learning the ropes of the camper from YouTube, relatives with campers, and once in a while even from the camper manual. I have successfully unhitched, leveled, put on license plates and found the spare tire. We tried out the refrigerator—it kept the beer cold.

The maiden voyage will be 35 miles tops to get the kinks out. At that point, I'll have to back into a camping site. Oh no. Poor trees.

—Journals in June—

Flailing

I turn on the reading lamp next to the bed. Within minutes a beetle is alternately clinging to and flailing against the window screen. It's an evening in June, near the solstice, the lingering bluish light having finally given in to darkness, bringing with it a whisper of cool air.

The lamp is between me and the window, only a foot from each, and I could throw my arm back and slap the screen with my hand.

But I don't. For I am fascinated by this hard-bodied, dark brown beetle. In turn, it's fascinated with light. The beetle buzzes, the sound vibrating from its wings. Then it scrapes the wire screen as it crawls closer to the light, the light it can't touch. Isn't seeing the light enough?

Right or wrong, since childhood I've called them June bugs. In the insect guide I'm happy to find the June beetle, or the ten-lined June beetle to be exact. The book tells me it's also known as a "june bug." Confirmation feels good.

But I know little about this night stalker of lights, other than it feeds in the darkness on roots of grasses and plants. It's an inch or so long and has chewing jaws.

So what does it want indoors, next to my light? Would it trade food for the warmth of the light bulb? Is that why it buzzes at the screen? It's trapped outdoors.

I'm trapped indoors, in the light of a late night, thinking of too much to do. My thoughts bang against the screen, wishing for the peaceful darkness of the outdoors.

The june bug and I, on opposite sides of the screen, both reaching for something. Both flailing in the summer night. I turn off the light and try to fall asleep. The june bug falls to the ground.

Possession

My wife and I own the hummingbird feeder and the contents therein outside the kitchen window. Or so we thought.

Over the past week a female ruby-throated hummingbird appears to have seized control of the feeder with red plastic perches and a clear bulb for the sweet liquid. This transfer of ownership has little effect on us but sure puts a dent in other hummingbirds' efforts to sip sugar water.

This tiny bird, not much bigger than my thumb but with a beak that even scares me a bit, spends an inordinate amount of time on a tiny twig protruding from a bush about 10 feet from the feeder. From this perch, Hulda—not her real name—has been on guard day after day.

Now and then she'll fly up into the nearby small maple tree's thick leaf cover, only to return to her guard post within minutes. Every so often, Hulda goes to the feeder and draws a drink. And then she's back to the twig.

If another hummingbird comes near, including the bit larger and more colorful males, Hulda goes into attack mode, dive bombing them until they surrender and fly away. And then hoggish Hulda returns to her post.

The other night when the June evening's darkness began gathering after 9 p.m., I could make out Hulda's silhouette, about 5 feet from our window. I got up a little after 5 o'clock the next morning and, yup, there she was in dawn's first light.

Sooner or later, as nature takes its course, Hulda will lay two eggs and give up guarding for incubating. Then, just maybe, someone else can get a drink.

Summer

So it's June already. Kids are off the hook from school, and now they hook up worms. Bigger kids—that would be adults—are thinking of playing hooky, but the weedy garden and peeling paint say otherwise, not to mention the lawn.

Bluegills are biting while ferns spread among the blooming wild geraniums. The sky is as blue as the leaves are green. One color against the other, complementing each other.

It's the month of the longest days, light arriving by 5 a.m., sunsets edging up against 9 p.m. The Milky Way stretches across the night sky. The orb-weaver spider spins its tale in the dew of a warm sunrise as herons take off on fishing trips, and deer and raccoons sneak home from a night out.

There are strawberries for your sweet tooth and wild roses for your sweetheart. The slate-gray catbird sings some other bird's song in the low bushes. I stumble upon a fawn, its brown eyes as big as its white spots, as if amazed by its new world.

The summer solstice eases upon us, the sun taking its most northerly path, from sunrise in the northeast to sunset in the northwest. So what to do with the "longest" day of the year? Look for agates in the storm-washed creek, and then spot Jupiter and Saturn as the sky finally begins to darken?

Sunrise. Share it with a cup of coffee on the porch, with birdsong the only sound? Or with a fishing rod on the smooth lake, the silence briefly broken by the plop of the bait rippling the water, and the call of a loon in the distance?

Sunset. Should I sit quietly watching a deer on silent hooves pick its way along emerging corn rows to query my presence? Or should I be on the trout stream at dusk, watching brookies break the surface for the latest hatch, and for my fascination if not my imitation?

And the long hours between dawn and dusk, what about them? Watch a catbird at the birdbath? Walk a trail while noting the brambles with green, budding blackberries? Should I mow lawn or drive through the country to smell fresh-mown hay? Perhaps I'll follow a bumblebee or butterfly, look for a walking stick—one the insect, the other a walking aid—then check the bluebird nest.

I feel the solstice, the tilting of the hemisphere, the assurance that the sun is tracing the correct path before it turns ever so slowly toward autumn. Is there a solstice in my life? Have I found the course of most light as I connect the natural world with my inner self?

On this day, there's plenty of time to find out.

9

Spittlebugs and Bobolinks

S kunk smell wafted through the house just before bedtime. On a stuffy June night, air had to be begged through the window screen, but the skunk odor had no trouble getting in. The problem was quickly solved with closing windows and switching to conditioned air.

The skunk, however, had a bigger problem. A skunk normally sprays only in life-threatening situations or when life ends. At the point of death a skunk may release its musk one last time in a futile act of protection. On this humid night, a skunk had met some deadly highway encounter under a waxing gibbous moon.

It's summer. Spittlebug froth hangs in alfalfa and tansies. From the spittlebug nymph's foamy fortress hangs memories of haying days. Though I don't remember spittlebugs, or their adult version froghoppers, doing any real damage, I do recall my dad looking at an alfalfa field with the small white clumps of spit-like moisture and saying something about "those dang spittlebugs."

Back then I observed nature but don't recall having appreciation for or knowledge of nature's intricacies. I wonder if children ever do, or need to. They observe with an innocent wonder and tuck the picture away, coming back to it years later when they find the words to match the memory.

And so it wasn't until years later that I learned that the nymph of the spittlebug is protected inside the frothy mass of spittle, the size of a piece of popcorn, for up to two months. Then a green bug emerges.

What a bug it is, capable of jumping two feet in the air. The quarter-inch spittlebug is said to be the best jumper among bugs with a vertical leap of up to 27 inches. Though the nymph stage of the spittlebug can stress plants and stunt growth, the adult bug can do little damage to a hayfield crop.

I walked into a hayfield this week. A pair of bobolinks flew across the grasses, their melodic notes trailing in their wake. This grassland bird sang more memories of haying days, those days when hayfields weren't cut until late June, giving the bobolink a chance at ground nesting. When hay cutting in early June became the norm, bobolinks began disappearing from the farming landscape.

But the bobolinks are back on our land after a decade of allowing the grasses to grow, unharvested, in a conservation program, followed by years of renting to a farmer who for whatever reason doesn't cut hay until July. It's all good for the bobolinks.

It's hard to describe the melody of this bird, which appears to be wearing a tuxedo backwards as it tinkles harp-like fairy music. Henry David Thoreau offered, "This flashing, tinkling meteor bursts through the expectant meadow air, leaving a train of twinkling notes behind."

To think the bobolink came 6,000 miles, from wintering in the sprawling grasslands of southwestern Brazil to sing to me on a day in June. I'm quite honored. If nesting is successful, the young bobolinks will make their first trip to Brazil, leaving with their parents as early as August.

Before that, the bobolinks will feed on bugs in the summer grasses. And, yes, they will feed on spittlebugs, which feed on the alfalfa, which hides the bobolinks' ground nest from predators, including egg-eating skunks. It's quite the circle of life, and death, in summer.

Like So Many Summer Fields

July – August

In 1969 I was 15, a teenage speck in the hayfields of summer days, waiting for summer nights, waiting for a time when the road was mine.

The fields were fresh air, open spaces and an unescapable sweaty sentence all rolled into windrows of hay that needed attention before any baseball game or date. I hoped for rain, though that would only delay the inevitable.

Thirty years go by. I walked through those fields in the rain in July. I heard a Jackson Browne song, the verse, "*Looking back on the years gone by like so many summer fields.*" Wet grasses of timothy, red clover, and fescue soaked my boots and pants legs.

I was looking back. I had a hand in what these fields had become. I ordered the mixture of grass seeds to meet Conservation Reserve Program (CRP) requirements a year after my father died. For years prior, a neighbor—a childhood friend—had rented the cropland from my parents.

But the rental agreement ended. I secured a CRP contract; we'd get paid for letting the land sit idle in tall grasses. The man came from the feed mill, spread seeds on 22 acres and was gone. Broadcast planting. First time ever on our farm, and it worked.

It was the right path financially. It was also the right path in that it satisfied my desire, my perceived responsibility, to provide habitat for birds and critters. Perhaps the grassland birds would return, most notably the ground-nesting bobolink.

Not all agreed. My childhood friend, classmate and neighbor, and then a successful farmer, urged me not to idle the land for a check from the government. However, he couldn't fiscally justify renting it anymore for annual crops.

We stood on the road next to the fields on a pretty summer's day, he the farmer who had followed in his father's footsteps, I the newspaper reporter who had gone to college. I listened without debate as he remained steadfast in his cropland argument. A month later, he died, crushed beneath his tractor in a hayfield. A hilly hayfield. His years gone by too fast, ending in a summer field.

I return to these fields often. They are no longer in conservation reserve, instead rented by an organic beef farmer who chooses not to bale hay until July, year after year. I watch the tall grass sway in the breeze in June, and I watch bobolinks, their nesting season safe from the sickle. The sweet-singing bird has returned here in numbers, its undulating flight and song in rhythm with the gentle summer wind on the grasses.

The years have passed now like so many hay crops and bobolink nests in so many summers. I look back on my years of personal growth and harvest, and then the need to grow and harvest again if I'm fortunate, if I stay out of the rain and storms of life.

I strive for the perfect summer day. In his poem "Hay-Cutters," William Stafford wrote:

> *You try to hope the clouds away.*
> *"Some year we'll have perfect hay."*

10

Staying True to His Roots

This is a story about a man and his tree. It's about the power of nature and positive thinking. About vindication and hanging out in hammocks.

The story starts with a straight-line wind in the middle of a summer's night, bearing down like a locomotive in a Johnny Cash song. The storm raised havoc while it razed trees. Let's zero in on Jim's yard, where a 50-foot ash tree was on the ground when morning broke.

It broke Jim's heart. This was one of his hammock trees, where he lazes in the soft summer breeze thinking about, well, I don't know what Jim thinks about, and I don't want to know. He's a free thinker.

The tree's fall crushed only the garden. A clump of roots and dirt, six feet across, stuck out of the ground at the base of the uprooted tree.

What to do, pondered Jim.

"I decided this was a manly opportunity to buy another power tool. So down to the manly store to pick out a chainsaw," said Jim.

Then Jim called me. We revved up our chainsaws like twin fiddles on steroids and sent wood chips into the summer air. I had a truckload of firewood. Jim had a 12-foot bare tree trunk angling upward, like a missile disguised in bark, the diamond-shaped bark of white ash.

Jim stared at the missile. "The idea to upright the tree came at that point," said Jim, though the basis for such a thought was probably born years ago in his free-wheeling college days. "When I shared the idea with Wendy, she gave me the wife look that says, *'I love you dear, but are you crazy?'*"

Jim searched elsewhere for positive reaction but found only skepticism. "Do you know how heavy that is?" "You'll never move it." "Why do you want to do that?" Some didn't say anything. They just walked away before they were enlisted in an act of failure.

But a man and his dream, or a man and the tree where he dreams, are hard to pry apart. Jim's brother said the tree would never move. But blood runs deeper than tree roots, so the brother agreed to help put a two-ton car jack under the stump and pump the handle.

The tree moved. Moved upward in fact. And so, the inspired Stavran boys, who probably snapped off ash saplings in wayward childhood days, began tree-raising, pumping and bracing until the trunk was at a 70-degree angle.

The car jack could do no more. A come-along winch hooked to a Blazer bumper moved only the Blazer. The tree balked in its awkward position. Nonbelievers came around again to pronounce the project hopeless. Someone asked if they could have the tree for firewood. Wendy said they could, and she thought about throwing Jim in with the deal, for this had become his Moby Dick.

But at the height of his frustration, as he considered sawing down his dream, Jim had one last idea. Down at Kev's Service, Kevin Ashland (no pun intended) listened, smiled and jumped into his tow truck.

Ashland hooked the ash, blocked the wheels and started to rewind cable. The tow truck didn't move. The tree did move. It was soon upright. Jim took a victory lap of vindication, then packed dirt around the tree's base before he and the ash settled in for winter.

In spring, the tree stayed upright in the soft ground and began sprouting twigs and branches and leaves. The bird house went back up in time for wrens to nest. Then the hammock was strung for Jim's summer rest.

A lesson in perseverance? Perhaps. Faith? Maybe. Or just a stubborn man getting lucky? Jim philosophized, "Even the mighty oak tree was once a nut that held its ground."

—Journals in July—

Smokey's Morning

One of my dogs gets up with the birds. On some mornings he simply sits on the edge of the deck and watches the birds and whatever else is moving in the dawning of the day.

I often look at him sitting there, so calm and composed, and wonder what he's seeing and hearing, and, though impossible to ever know, "what is he thinking?". Is the early morning as reflective for  him as it is for me as the first sunlight sprinkles through the birch leaves and pine boughs? Is he shaking sleep from his eyes? Does he enjoy a new day starting slowly and quietly?

A finch comes to the feeder above him. In the nearby pine tree, crows discuss their morning carrion routes. A gray squirrel balances on the utility wire above the lawn. Smokey watches the squirrel intently but makes no move, feels no need to chase since the brother that eggs him on is still in the house, sleeping.

I join Smokey, sit down on the deck tight against him, and together we watch the new day starting. I practice seeing. A hummingbird flies from the blooming bergamot at the base of the deck and alights on a birch branch. To pick out a hummingbird on a branch is indeed an exercise in seeing.

The resident chipmunk pokes its head out of the firewood pile. The squirrel takes another high-wire trip. A robin lands in the rock garden, and Smokey's head rises just a bit. A few hours later he'll chase all the players in this scene. But for now, in dawn's light, it's as if even Smokey is amazed by morning rising from the dark.

I've heard that a sign of inner tranquility is the ability to hear the sound of the sun going down. I think my dog hears the sound of the sun coming up.

In Focus

It's a quiet summer morning, just after sunrise, the golden sphere climbing behind the pines after resting on the horizon ever so briefly. It's an unruffled beginning to a day with the promise of humid sizzle later, which ironically will be aided by this same soft sun of morning.

My father died on such a summer's day. As the long hospital ordeal played out over spring and early summer, it was often bittersweet—the ending of his pain but also my ongoing pain of his impending death.

I discovered something soothing that summer that I have never been quite able to explain. On my 60-mile trips to the hospital, I saw the beauty and wonder of the countryside like I had never noticed it.

The focus and detail were incredibly sharp. The tree-topped hills climbed above farm fields of emerald green corn and tannish hay raked into perfect rows. Dark creeks meandered through green pastures. The shades of green were greater than my soul of blues.

Now, on this peaceful morning I look out from the deck of my mother-in-law's home. I am the caregiver at this hour, in another summer filled with uncertainty and sadness, with death in the wings. Again, my field of vision is in keen focus, most notably on the towering bur oak tree rising past the deck to its wide canopy, more than 75 feet high.

I see in detail the scaly patterns of deeply-furrowed bark, the way the branches angle and jut away from the trunk, how the leaves are backlit by the sun. As the breeze picks up, the leaves turn over to show a whitish backside.

In the midst of my pain, once again, comfort comes softly and subtly in the vivid view of creation.

Hidden Nests

The catbird was calling me out with its cawing meow. It was persistent and a bit louder and pronounced as I drew closer and closer to the 15-foot-high wild plum tree. And then I saw it, what the catbird was protecting and why it was protesting. Not far above my head was a nest occupied by another catbird, presumably on eggs.

I slowly backed away from the first catbird nest I'd ever seen, though I often look for one in the bushes bordering our yard. Catbirds come to our birdbath, so they must nest nearby, I always figured but couldn't confirm.

It happens every summer about this time. I'm consumed with a backyard chore and then, when taking a moment to look around at nature all around, I see a bird's nest. It's usually in plain sight but out of my tunnel sight.

One summer it was a cedar waxwing nest low in the apple tree near the garage. I had mowed the lawn there through the spring and early summer but had not seen the nest. In late July, while taking a reading on the apples, I was startled to see little beaks and feathered faces pointed at me. Cedar waxwing chicks, all nestled up.

Another time it was a robin's nest in the lilac branches, the robin staring down at me while on its second clutch of eggs. Last summer near this same spot but in the box elder tree a robin's nest caught my eye, if only because from the bottom of the nest dangled a UPC symbol.

Was this a lazy robin that went to the hardware store and bought a nest? The nest was unoccupied, so I climbed a ladder to check out the seven-inch long plastic tag with the barcode among the construction of grass and mud.

The tag was off a Keller medium-duty step ladder. The robin was gone. The ladder was who knows where. For the heck of it, I tucked the UPC tag back into the nest. Maybe it will be recycled nest material next spring.

11

The Wait for New Life

This was the summer I would see the snapping turtle's eggs hatch. It was May 26 when I came across the female snapper oozing out eggs in the loose gravel on a trail bordering a swamp. Snapping turtles have sharp vision despite small eyes. So the turtle had a good look at me as I circled it. She paid no mind.

I counted my steps north to the nearest landmark tree, then continued my run. The nest was marked. I would check it throughout the summer.

Exactly two weeks earlier, on May 12, I had called my older brother to wish him a happy 66th birthday. "Are you on Route 66 today?" I asked when he answered. He laughed, "I guess I am."

Turtle eggs take time to hatch. In these parts, three months is about right, though hatching can be sped along by hot weather. Though I would begin watching the eggs in earnest in August, I would check the nest every other day throughout the summer to see if a raccoon or skunk dug into the nest, which is often the fate of turtle eggs.

It was a wet summer, a hot summer. Deer flies pestered me as I ran past the turtle eggs, still buried safely and just out of the wheel path of all-terrain vehicles. The trail of the tail of the big snapper—perhaps a 25-pounder—faded in the gravel throughout the summer, slowly erasing the turtle's path to and from the nest.

Wild roses were blooming in the yard as I walked to the mailbox in June. There was an anniversary card from my brother, the best man at our outdoor wedding.

Snapping turtles are said to have a belligerent disposition when on land. That's when we mostly encounter them, when they leave the water to lay eggs. Who wouldn't be belligerent when fat with eggs and laboring under a heavy shell? Further, snappers don't move well on land.

On the Fourth of July, a Sunday, another inch and a half of rain fell in the early morning. I called my brother just to talk. Rain was headed his way. Late July brought more heavy rain. Raspberries were ripe along the trail, and now there were more monarch butterflies than deer flies. The turtle nest remained free of predation.

The female snapper lays at least a couple of dozen eggs. Imagine how small a baby snapper is. Not much more than half a basketball would fit in the hole the turtle excavates. In that nest, seven inches at its deepest point, are about 25 little turtles, each in a white egg smaller than a chicken egg. I have seen baby snappers, their bodies the size of a matchbook.

My brother called on the last day of July to compliment me on a photo of mine he had seen published. We talked for a time. There were plans of getting together in September.

In early August, as Jupiter cut a bright circle in the night sky, I anticipated new life. I wanted to see the turtles hatch. I ran every day to the spot. The first week or so of August was hot. The turtles would hatch soon.

My brother died on the 10th day of August. Life ended so suddenly for him that it took away the collective breath of our family. The weeks that followed were a blur. With what little time and ambition I had, I tried to run, but ended up walking in tears, and not far enough to the turtle eggs.

A month later, with some sadness lifting, I was up for a run of normal course and distance. The nest was no more. The spot was a small crater sprinkled with bits of white shells. I couldn't see it, but somewhere there was new life.

—Journals in August—

Clouds

When I was a small boy, I'd lay on my back next to the barn's silo on summer days and watch clouds pass by the silver dome. They were puffy white clouds in a blue sky, and amusing illusions in a boy's eyes.

My fascination with clouds would only heighten as I studied their flight and ever-changing shapes. *Amusing illusions.* A cloud would appear as an animal, say a dragon or dog, but the head and tail would grow or shrink before my eyes. And then what I had seen as a dragon or dog would suddenly be all different, twisting my imagination as it transformed into a bird or maybe even a state. Look, Montana is flying!

I could also stare long enough to make the clouds stand still. This would create another illusion, that of the silo moving, as in falling, which caught my attention real fast. I'd close my eyes to block out the fear and then open them again to let the clouds continue on.

Where were the clouds going? How far and how fast? Would they circle the globe or dissipate over the neighbor's hill? Would a cloud that looked like a bear above me take on that same form 10 or 100 miles away?

I looked at clouds again the other day through the eyes of an adult. Squinting back to a child's view of the sky I saw two dogs in the clouds. One dog was sitting looking away from me, the other stretched out and pushing a paw toward the sitting dog. It all changed so quickly, when the sitting dog suddenly became a poodle's head.

I once had a poodle, and now I saw a poodle in the sky. Was it mine? Maybe. My poodle in the sky, and a little kid in my heart.

Magically Cool

It was the hottest day of the summer so far, this day in late July. So I put on running shoes and shorts and started down the trail. I was running into, if not quite buying into, the heat index.

The trail of dirt and cinder was cooled, by as much as 10 degrees, in the splotches of shade beneath overhanging branches of poplars, maples and oaks. Ferns swayed at my side to the whims of the warm breeze.

My destination was not far—enjoying a little heat being one thing and challenging it to the extreme quite another. Clutching a thermometer, I headed straight for the creek, just shy of a mile away.

The air temperature was 94°F. I took my time on the mile to the stream, where I slipped off the main trail and followed a short path to the water. To almost another world, one that was heavily shaded, the cool air suspended above the tiny stream rippling away from a shallow pool.

I eased the thermometer into the water, secured it between two rocks, and then instinctively cupped the cool water in my hands and splashed it on my head, neck and shoulders.

I sat down, relieved by the breeze licking at the sweat and stream water on my skin. This spot was magically cool; the brook trout already knew. The water was 58°F, nearing but half a dozen degrees below a brook trout's summer tolerance high mark.

Blending into the murky shade, I watched tiny trout dart about the pool. Reluctantly, I finally walked out of the cool, damp cove and into the hot, sunny afternoon.

Summer Regrets

August has come around with its promise of blackberries, goldenrod and spider webs, all reminders of summer slipping away and what I didn't do. In my summer of some regrets, I didn't catch enough fish, take that marathon bicycle ride on a forest trail, sleep in a tent, or watch enough sunsets fade into murky darkness of flapping bats and the first specks of stars and planets.

There's still time, I suppose, but this summer hasn't felt long and lazy. Seems there was not enough time to get lost in summer's haze and all those hours of daylight. It's as if summers are shorter.

Can't be. Nature all around us hasn't changed. It takes the same number of days on the nest to coax songbird chicks out of eggs. Whitetail mothers patiently hide their spotted fawns for weeks until the gangly-legged youngsters are old enough to tag along. Moon phase cycles are a constant 29½ days. The Big Dipper slowly pours. Nothing rushes sunset.

I slowed time twice this week by simply sitting outdoors, once in a forest clearing next to a hayfield, and another time on a lakeshore. I had no phone, and imagined I had no place to be, no one waiting for me.

The woodland was quiet except for the occasional buzzing of a fly. Butterflies of all sizes and colors danced among the black-eyed Susans and red clover. Suddenly a chunky hawk, with rusty breast and white-banded black tail, soared silently over the clearing. I did not know what it was—a broad-winged hawk was my guess—but counted it as a reward for sitting quietly.

Along the lakeshore a mallard hen swam past with one lone duckling in tow, the young one struggling in the hen's wake. Why only one? The hen cut the water smoothly, effortlessly, while the duckling bounced awkwardly, its feet churning hard beneath the water to keep up.

I walked away, now determined to keep up too. Keep up with summer. It may take more slowing down.

12

Drawn to the Listening Point

In the stillness tonight I heard the past. Wilderness guide Sigurd Olson wrote that each of us has a listening point, "Some place of quiet where the universe can be contemplated with awe."

I come to this place often, always looking and listening for something. As a farm boy I was looking for a tree branch crashed on the fence or listening for a cow's newborn calf. Some 40 years later I steal away in the middle of the night just to be here again, looking and listening.

I remember staring into leafless trees in the fall, looking for the squirrel my dad had already seen. And when I saw it my dad steadied me as I settled the small rifle to my shoulder and took aim.

Those trees are the backdrop tonight behind a flickering campfire. I listen for a noise but there is none, save for the crackle of wood releasing trapped moisture. I settle into a chair and face the northeast where the sky opens up from this small clearing off the corner of a hayfield.

I'm here to look for the Perseid meteors of August. It's cool and damp, so damp that by the time I leave at 2 a.m., the lenses on my camera and binoculars will be drenched. I haven't sat more than a couple of minutes when a meteor races across the sky. It's 12:13 a.m. This will be a good meteor night, I tell myself.

I wait for the next flash. My mind wanders to my childhood dog—his grave is just down the trail among the tall maples and oaks where he and I would hunt squirrels. The squirrels now chew acorns above his resting spot, the shells dropping on the concrete headstone of a single word lettered in agates, "Rusty."

Another streak halts my flow of memories. And then it's gone, somewhere behind the hill to the northeast. I fall back into reverie, to my college days of rushing home to these woods to take photos of leaves, hunt deer, help with firewood. I'd listen for the whine of the chainsaw and follow the sound to my dad.

I still cut firewood here, but now alone. The wood feeds the small stove at home. It's only a secondary heat—a bit of a luxury—providing a cozy breezeway for my watch on winter. I work in the woods by choice while thinking of those before me who worked the woods out of necessity.

Three or four more meteors splash across the sky in no particular pattern. One streaks sideways, right to left, cutting through the Big Dipper and burning out near due north. Another comes close to Cassiopeia, the W-shaped queen high in the northeast.

But then, after a few more meteors, the Perseid shower stops like a faucet turning off. I lean back from the camera on a tripod and stare at the Milky Way. I look to my right into the dark woods, to where a deer trail goes under the best hunting stand I ever had in the forked trunk of a maple tree. A storm snapped off one of the trunks, slapped around my nailed boards, ruined my point of ambush.

These days I look and listen for more than deer. I'm drawn here by wildflowers, monarch butterfly pupae hanging from milkweed leaves, and the chance to see a scarlet tanager. And for butternuts, blackberries and crab apples. I look for where my parents had their maple sap boiler, and where those who cleared the land piled rocks a hundred years ago.

Tonight, between meteors, I look at the stars. How many thousand stars, how many jewels in the sky? I wish I could have viewed the sky from here a century ago. The August constellations and Milky Way haven't changed, but the sky was surely darker, the stars surely brighter.

As I leave, one last meteor burns out above bright Capella, the star dominating the northeastern sky near the horizon. Capella doesn't flinch, only twinkles, perhaps in awe. I know I am.

The Color of Resignation

September – October

It's 8:26 a.m. Five minutes to go. Five minutes before autumn arrives on this 22nd day of this ninth month. On a woodland trail—an abandoned railway—I intersect a road, look to my right and see the far hillside, half-colored with autumn.

On the narrow corridor, the season is softly, almost apologetically, showing muted greens and browning ferns. A few small maples display a few reddening leaves. But for the most part, summer is reluctant to leave on this warm first day of autumn.

I check my watch for the exact moment of the autumnal equinox at 8:31 a.m. It arrives, announced by a crow cawing in the distance. I look behind me to see a squirrel, a couple of hours into its day of harvest and caching. I glance over my shoulder at the sun through the leaves, the sun that is now standing directly over the equator in Bogota in South America or Singapore in the Far East.

So here it is, autumn arriving in the smooth summery light of September, the light that Sarah Helen Whitman wrote of a century ago: "In the soft light of an autumnal day, when summer gathers up her robes of glory and like a dream of beauty glides away."

But the glide is slow, so tells me the summer wildflowers along the trail, including the yellow and orange of butter and eggs, the white of bladder campion and the purple of red clover. Autumn is, however, squeezing in with red sumac and blue asters.

I am pulled into an autumnal frame of mind as I cross a footbridge over the creek, its water carrying away a few colored leaves. Now I want autumn, want to wander in it, to where the multicolored brook trout spawns, where the apples blush and where old logs wait for young grouse.

I free a red leaf and stare at the simple brilliance in my hand, the brilliance of which poet Thomas W. Parsons wrote: "September strews the woodlot o'er with many a brilliant color; the world is brighter than before, why should our hearts be duller."

Suddenly, the season we wait for is half over. It's October. The breeze pauses along the fence line, perhaps to wonder at the same maple trees draped in hues of yellow, orange and red that have captured my gaze. The breeze picks up, rustling the leaves against the blue sky.

My mood swings from inspiration to a hint of frustration as I ask myself why this woodland wonderland has to fade so soon? I am anxious and gracious. I settle on the inspiring positive, tracing the soft flow of the land on which autumn paints its colors before it lets go of another season.

Suddenly my mood has softened, and I feel a sweet contentment in me, and in the day, watching nature in easy resignation to its last act before winter. Perhaps the end of a season so beautiful but so short gives us pause to consider our own end. If autumn all around us is so glorious, wouldn't we wish for the same when our personal harvest nears an end?

And so we realize how fortunate we are to be wrapped in another fall, watching how gracefully nature moves on. And keeps moving on, with purpose. A leaf falls, but finds its place on the forest floor. We would best be served to accept the same cycles of life and find our place.

13

To the River of Renewal

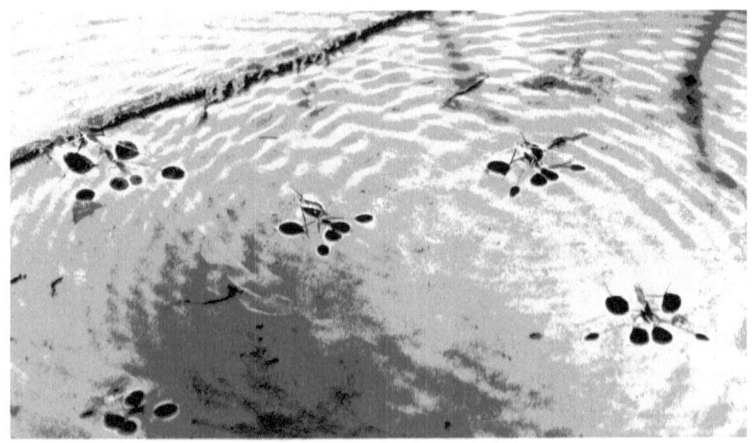

Nothing is going to rush past here today. Hay River is moving so slowly that I wonder if there's a flow at all. The boy in me reaches down for a stick and tosses it into the water. The stick begins to move, painstakingly slow. I wonder when, even if, it will reach the sleepy village five miles downstream.

Slowness has not been a part of my life of late. That's the point of being here, in a river valley of farm country and town roads rising and falling with the flow of the land. I'm looking for something not rushed—a young deer staring at me, a blue heron stalking a fish, a frog half in, half out of the warm pooled water.

I've found the river. This is where I'll slow down and observe something, anything, sights and sounds that I can bundle into words for others, all the while occupying a nook of contentment. I recall a sentence from an outdoors writer struggling to connect the words: "You cannot write about the outdoors unless you are out there."

So I'm out there. At the river. I stumble down the weedy bank next to the bridge and crawl carefully over a stiff barbed-wire fence. I struggle through the thick brush to find the river, which was so easily visible from the bridge. The trails are those of deer. I'm bent over, following a path where deer only have to lower their heads. The tag alders are so thick I'm getting only glimpses of the river.

I reach an opening to the water and toss the stick just beyond the low bank. The river is slow, but how slow? Perhaps a single mile per hour? My later research confirms that one mph is a good estimate for a sluggish river. But I have my doubts that the stick is going to reach the bluffs of Prairie Farm, five miles away, in five hours.

I want to follow the stick, but instead stop by a side pool where what appears to be giant mosquitos are racing back and forth atop the stagnant water. Long-legged and gangly, they bounce off each other as they rapidly propel forward and backward.

They are common water striders, an insect with six legs and no wings, about half an inch long. The two hind legs are used for steering, the middle legs for rowing, the shorter front legs for sensing, grabbing, and holding food. Striding, as in taking long steps, doesn't fit what the water striders are doing. They glide, scoot, skim or skate atop the water, as fast as a couple of feet per second.

Against the tannish, silty river bottom, with the sun over my shoulder, the striders create a shadow of an elongated body with six roundish blobs. This puzzles me until I read that the dots of shade are made by the strider's feet dimpling the water's surface. The dots are dimples.

The river is in no hurry. Not so the water striders which have a lifespan of 15 days. They rush to eat and reproduce on a river that is in no mood to rush anywhere or anything. That is why I'm here, to arrest my rush. The frenetic pace of the water striders is only a brief distraction.

I asked of the lazy river and received the means to slow down, recalibrate, reflect, find inspiration, and to mark an anniversary. It was 50 years ago this summer that, by chance at a garage sale, I picked up a book, drawn to it only by its stark cover of trees reflected in water, along with the title, *Pilgrim at Tinker Creek*.

Something drew me to that book that day, to Annie Dillard's writings tracing a year of her explorations and study of nature. Had I not found the book I doubt I would be at the river today, at least not to simply observe, to watch 15 minutes in a water strider's 15-day life, to note the jewel-weed at my feet and the oak leaves above me, from which comes the song of the Eastern phoebe, urging the river on. And on it goes.

—Journals in September—

Gifts

The sun shouldered its way over the horizon and soon found a portal in the pine boughs through which to shoot a ray my way. Coffee in hand, I suddenly noticed a soft yet distinctive shadow on the glass patio door, the shadow of a hummingbird hovering next to a fuchsia plant.

The scene played out without any attraction hanging from a string or suctioned to the glass. The sun was sending a ray from 93 million miles away to give me free window artistry, if only for a moment. The hummingbird was feeding on the flower 12 feet away on the deck. The bird suddenly buzzed away, and the sunray met up with the pine branches. The shadow was gone.

I took a sip of coffee and thought of how easily the gifts of nature, and of life, come and go, and come again if we keep looking, keep hoping. No sooner had the shadow disappeared than I noticed a robin battling for balance as it gorged on the orange berries of the mountain ash tree.

The hummingbird and robin were feeling a tug from the south. It was a tug telling them to feed, feed now and feed heavily. Soon there will be miles to be made; the sun is showing up later every September morning.

This slipping away of daylight was subtle at first. August's string of days with mesmerizing sameness lulls one into an endless summer state of mind. But summers are never endless, and the hummingbirds and robins will soon be someone else's shadow, someone else's gift.

I will look to September, however, for gifts yet to come: Goldenrod blooming, blackbirds gathering. I will gather my thoughts, in September. A chill in the night, sun warming the afternoon. I'll have warm memories, in September.

Painted leaves and faded tansies. Lingering butterflies and easy breezes. Red apples and blue asters, old shotguns and canoe paddles, wood smoke at the cabin and frost on the pumpkin, in September.

Velvet curls from deer antlers, woolly bears curl in fright. I'll curl up with a good book, in September. Full Harvest Moon, northern lights and southern flights. I'll look to the sky, in September.

Doomed

Sometimes I don't want to know. Don't want to see it, don't want to hear it. Sometimes I wish what Greek philosopher Heraclitus said applied to nature's missteps and tragedies: "Nature is wont to hide herself."

A monarch butterfly twitched and shuddered on the blacktop, dying in the sunshine of early autumn. One wing was sliced away, by a car, I assumed.

Missing a wing, the butterfly was doomed. There would be no long migration flight to overwinter in the volcanic mountain region of central Mexico. I carried the butterfly to the grass beneath the bushes and laid it down to die in the shade of fading greenness.

A few days later there was a bird, crouched in fear with wings spread slightly on the ground. It was unable to muster any other effort to escape my approach. I was not a danger of any kind, simply a runner on a trail. The bird didn't know. It didn't matter. It couldn't move.

The bird was on the side of the packed gravel trail near a footbridge. It was unable to even crawl into the grass and leaves. I made a mental note of the location so I could stop on my way back, though not knowing how I could help; human intervention regarding sick or injured songbirds rarely turns out well.

I crossed the footbridge and made 10 minutes north, turned around and covered the 10 minutes south, back to the bridge. My feet plopped on the wooden planks in the otherwise silent afternoon. I reached the gravel on the other side and looked down to my right.

The bird was dead. It had died in the 20 minutes I was gone. I knelt down, knowing I could not have helped this bird. I handled it carefully, reverently, determining it was a juvenile gray catbird by its slate color and long tail.

There are many reasons butterflies and songbirds die, and die in alarming numbers, especially the young of the year. I left the bird on the quiet, shaded trail. I paused a moment, then ran away from the facts of nature.

Missing

I had lost the pry bar. It went missing somewhere in the 40 acres of this woods that is my outdoor sanctuary, where I cut firewood and hunt for ruffed grouse and deer while watching the natural world pass by slowly and sanely.

The pry bar is six feet long, heavy at 16 pounds but lean and mean. I purchased it for $5 at a yard sale 20 some years ago. Ever since it has helped me argue with logs, urging them to roll over so I can reduce them to 17-inch chunks of firewood.

I was always careful to set the pry bar upright against a tree when not in use, knowing full well if I laid it down it could disappear on the forest floor, which I fear had happened in a moment of carelessness.

So I searched that forest floor for nearly two years, before leaf fall, through deer hunting and into early winter if there was no snow. And I searched in spring, walking across the flattened leaves after snowmelt. I even offered a cash reward during deer hunting for any family members or friends stumbling across it.

It didn't turn up. I recalled and retraced every spot where I had cut firewood about the time the pry bar went missing. But nothing. I became resigned to the strong possibility I would never find it, or that when I did it would be 20 years down the road when I can only walk the woods, not work the woods.

I promised myself I wouldn't curse the late find but instead pass the tool along to a younger woodcutter fortunate to have the same woodland opportunities as I have had.

But it was only two years down the road when one day with spring coming on fast and winter retreating with equal rapidity, I was surveying the woodlot for winter damage that I could turn into firewood. And there it was, the pry bar leaning against a tree.

I couldn't believe my eyes. Jubilation! I had set the bar so upright that it was hard to see against the dark tree trunk. It was also on the opposite side from the tote road I had walked so many times.

Reunited, we went back to working together, the pry bar and me. My work companion had been faithful, staying put where I put it, waiting through the seasons for me to return. Someday someone else will own the pry bar, but not before they know the story.

14

Settlers and Caretakers

Weighing on my mind amid the color of this October afternoon is a big book and a big chunk of wood, both packing plenty of pounds. I crash the splitting maul into the wood but there is no split. The wood has taken on too much rain of late and now weighs 50 pounds. It needs today's sunshine and warm breeze, and then more days of the same.

The book weighs 10 pounds and has more than 1,100 pages. I've only read a few pages in this 1922 edition of

History of Barron County. Those pages have plenty to do with these woods where I toil on firewood.

I'm on a piece of land our family calls "Breen's," my parents having purchased the 60 acres from neighbors Carl and Alma Breen in the 1950s. The land of half fields, half woodlot pasture was added to my parents' 90-acre dairy farm.

The 60 acres remain in the family. This place of woods and grassy fields is yesterday's childhood, today's refuge and hopefully tomorrow's days of retirement enjoyment. It's also pioneering history.

Breen's is part of the story of Norwegian immigrant Louis J. Breen, who left Osterdalen, Norway, in 1868 as a 20-year-old and landed in Minnesota's Fillmore County where he took on painting and farming jobs. Then he packed up again in 1875 to claim a piece of land in Wisconsin's Barron County.

The book tells me the piece of land was "all wild" when Louis Breen arrived in Section 32 of Arland Township. But he and his family cut trees and brush, piled up rocks, pulled and burned stumps, and built cabins and barns in a clearing, establishing "a good farm with comfortable and sightly buildings, and well-fenced and well-tilled acres."

Louis Breen died at age 59 in 1908, with the farm passing to his son Carl, who was well along in years by the time my parents purchased their first farm across the road in the early 1950s. At some point, Carl and his wife, Alma, thought it wise to unload the 60 acres on the same side of the road as my parents' farm.

And so here I am, 70 years since the addition of Breen's, cutting firewood and clearing trails on an October afternoon. There is no way I can feel the hardships and hard work here of those in the late 1800s. I'm clearing brush for walking and hunting trails, not for raising a crop and feeding a family. The firewood is not a necessity, just a cozy second source of heat in our city house.

I am not the settler, but I feel a caretaker responsibility for those who did settle the land. I could let the prickly ash, buckthorn, and maple saplings overrun the forest, and let the downed firewood trees go to waste. What would be the difference? The difference is that these woods and fields, these trails and the clearing in the woods, have served me and our family well for a long time. If I am the careful caretaker, won't this land continue to serve my hopes and dreams, and soothe my soul, and then do the same for others someday?

There are always butternuts and berries here, deer and grouse, too. There are campfires and a thousand stars. I hear pheasants cackle, watch the bobolink's flight over the field, and spy on coyotes and foxes who are looking for grouse and pheasants.

There are plenty of big maple trees here. Some of them, most notably one down in the corner by the rock pile, looked big when I was a kid 50 years ago. Today I squint in the slanting sunshine to study the sugar maple's dark branches and yellow leaves. I wonder if Louis and Carl Breen did the same on such a glorious October afternoon as they built a fence past the young maple, or sawed wood nearby.

In the ravines are huge boulders that the Breens bullied and pulled, with sweat and the help of horses harnessed to stone boats. Everywhere I look I realize the hard work that was done for me a century or more ago. To care for this land and to continue to make use of it is an easy job, a labor of love, a privilege. I'm not the settler, but caretaking settles my soul.

—Journals in October—

Apples

Five apples. That's all I could count as I circled the tree tucked inconspicuously off the trail in this woodland just beyond the city's edge.

Low brush scratched my bare legs as I stumbled beneath the branches, gazing upward in a break from my trail run. The apples were rather large, their species unknown to me.

Five apples. Soon to be three.

I knew this tree was here, having taken photos last winter of its brown and frozen apples wearing caps of snow and too high for deer to reach. Now in the heart of apple season there was only a handful of this season's apples on the old scraggly tree, well past its prime of production.

I first saw this tree years ago. The autumn discovery of an apple tree far away from buildings and roads always stirs my imagination. The red jewels are right there in front of me, but the tree's history is not as easy to see.

Am I standing where a farmstead once thrived decades ago? Was the apple tree in the backyard, or perhaps in the pasture or woodlot just beyond where I found what appeared to be the remnants of a building's foundation? If I poke further off the trail will I find more signs of a farm's crumbled past?

I imagine the tree was once harvested by someone who lived here or nearby. Harvested on splendid autumn days, the promise of apple pie and apple sauce in the pickers' hands. Did the farmers come here with gunny sacks, or was an apron simply folded up for a makeshift tote bag? Now the tree bears fruit with no idea for whom. Perhaps deer and birds, along with the occasional hiker who passes by.

I couldn't resist. The two largest and reddest of the five apples were within arm's reach. I snapped one off a twig, and the other apple tumbled to the ground. One for me, one for the deer.

I imagined a deer finding the apple later that day, like a child discovering a shiny penny on the sidewalk. I walked away, clutching my red prize, having added another small piece to the history of an old apple tree living out its days in near obscurity.

Solitude

In search of solitude and tranquility now more than ever, I took to the big woods in the afternoon. I went for the penetrating peace and quiet I believed could be found. But I also carried a shotgun in case a ruffed grouse flushed, tempting me to break the silence.

I've been here before. But not for some time had I sat and listened, hoping to hear nothing. I tried hard to hear something, not that I wanted to but just to prove I had found a place without noise. A dog barked in the distance now and then, a hunting dog I assumed. A couple of times a vehicle's engine groaned a bit along some hilly dirt road somewhere. Then it was quiet again.

The October woods filled my senses with the smell of fallen leaves which uttered not a sound. Even birds flitted silently from branch to branch. It was the loud peacefulness of the outdoors.

The silence was its own sound, that of the leaves coming down and the sun slicing through the exposed branches against a blue autumn sky. In the calming sigh of October, preparing for change, I decided that any encounter with a grouse would not rush me to raise my gun, but instead to simply listen to the propulsion of wings.

The peacefulness came over these woods long before I arrived and would remain long after I left. I got up to walk the trail. The quiet was softly disturbed only by my boots rustling the leaves. I imagined it created the similar soothing sound as what naturalist Sigurd Olson described as a "hypnotic swish" when his canoe paddle plied the still waters of the North Country.

In the vast silence, Olson observed, "There are moments when one seems suspended between heaven and earth."

I felt suspended in the big woods. I wondered who walked in this solitude before me, finding the same serenity. I know some of those hunters and hikers whose steps in later years slowed to match the pace of this place; they fell in line with their time.

And now I approach that time, to take my turn to walk the autumn woods with an untangled mind, when the world will be quieter and spin a bit more slowly. I hope.

Drumming

Despite my approach, the ruffed grouse held tight to its drumming log on an October afternoon. I decided not to take advantage in this uncharacteristic lull in vigilance of a bird that lives on the wary edge, always ready to flush from danger.

I had stopped the chainsaw while cutting firewood. The grinding whine of the saw was replaced by drumming, that John Deere tractor "putt-putt-putt" sound a ruffed grouse makes. The putts grew louder and more rapid over several seconds, culminating in a blurred roar before a couple of minutes of silence until the next session.

This drumming is more often heard in spring, when male grouse repeatedly announce their mating territory. With a downhill opening in one direction and escape cover to the rear, the grouse snaps its wings faster and faster, creating a sonic-booming muffled thumping.

But the drumming isn't limited to spring. In fall, it's thought the male ruffed grouse drums to persuade dispersed young grouse to find their own territory. Get off of my log!

The drumming was not far away. It finally got the best of me, so with shotgun in hand I began stalking my way toward the grouse, moving only during drumming to mask my steps in the leaves. Not more than a hundred yards away, after a climb out of a shallow gully, there it was, the grouse in classic drumming pose on a moldering log.

Sunshine highlighted the bird's erect black ruff circling its neck. The grouse stared at me as I stepped closer, my finger on the trigger in anticipation of a 20-gauge blast. I was now close enough to shoot the bird off the log or wait for it to flush, the sporting way, I guess.

I did neither. Suddenly, I didn't want to kill on this pretty fall afternoon, which had apparently so entranced the grouse that it didn't want to leave its drumming log. Now I wanted my camera, which I hadn't brought along as the hunter in me had trumped the photographer in me. I slowly stepped backwards and out of the grouse's view, and then rushed to my truck.

I returned with the camera only minutes later and began the stalk all over again. This time the grouse was on high alert, interesting in that I now was armed with a camera, not a gun. Its head lifted as its neck stretched, the forecast of flushing. I snapped a couple of quick photos.

The grouse took flight, a flush that produced enough moving air to send dry leaves upward, mixing with my visual memory of the bird's colors of reddish brown, grays and blacks, all in an intricate pattern of spots and bars.

I had a decent photo and a good feeling. The bird had the rest of the afternoon in the autumn woods. So did I. The chainsaw was waiting.

15

Sunsets and Chestnuts

Through no wishful thinking or design on our part, others' plight transformed into our delight as the red sun slipped toward the far shore of Lake Superior. I walked, with camera in hand, the 30 feet from our camper door to where the water softly splashed and danced on the shoreline rocks of Chequamegon Bay.

I was not the only one. Half a dozen folks were being pulled to the lakeshore, like a tide coming from land, on this early evening in September, a warm breeze riding across the bay. We were all being pulled to the show across the water on the western horizon.

The sun was settling down and taking on a complexion of orange and red, the color intensifying as the sphere neared the horizon. The sunset was filtered through a smoky haze we could not easily see or smell, nor fear any danger from on this soothing evening. The haze and ensuing soothing sunset were nevertheless the result of wild fires ravaging the Western states, a couple of thousand miles away, its smoke drifting eastward on the jet stream.

How could this peaceful, beautiful scene be the byproduct of fiery destruction so far away? I felt guilty. "Did you get a winner?" a woman asked as I clicked through the images on my camera. Perhaps, but the sunset's gift of beauty here was a tale of tragedy elsewhere. No winners in that elsewhere.

The red ball of sun slipped away. Night came and so did the stars. On our arrival at the campground I had taken a reading on directions, using my phone. I noted due north and used a landmark across the bay to remember, but now I wanted the stars to reaffirm it.

From the same spot I stood in the afternoon, at the base of the camper steps, I found Polaris, the North Star, with pointer help from the Big Dipper. Technology and the heavens were in perfect accord. Lights of a harbor town glowed across the bay from five miles away. Campfires flickered all around us.

The water was choppy the next afternoon as the wind picked up. Hardy sailors who knew something about reefed sails sped past in heavy chops. Wind on the bay was from the west, no doubt carrying more smoke our way. My wife and I walked along the shoreline trail to where trees and bushes hugging the shoreline sheltered us from the brisk breeze.

I turned my attention to the vegetation along the path. Every camping trip sooner or later comes to this. Soon I had a collection of plants and flowers in my mind, in my hand and on my camera, including bur marigolds in yellow, touch-me-nots in orange, crown vetch in whitish pink, and milkweed, still holding green pods this far north.

From one small tree I picked round fruit, the hull olive-colored and spiky. It was not familiar to me. Later at the picnic table I split the hull open to uncover two shiny dark brown nuts inside. I matched the findings with my field guide, determining the tree was a horse-chestnut.

I set the chestnuts aside and started the grill, started cooking on the shores of Gitche Gumee. Another clear evening descended upon Chequamegon Bay, another red sunset across the big water. Later, at the campfire, I stared into the flaring glow, thankful for flames that provide reflection, not destruction.

Sometimes the Best of Times

November — December

I was in a tree swaying to the rapid rhythm of November's chesty wind when it hit me. Not literally, though I suppose a weak branch could have let loose in a bold gust of wind and knocked me on the noggin.

What hit me was that my autumn of blue skies, dazzling leaves, calm afternoons, and migrating geese was over. All I could see and feel was fall ending. I saw it through bare branches as I stared in vain for a deer to appear. I felt a chill run through my body from the wind as clouds threatened the sun trying to slink away to the southwest.

There was little bird activity, though two chickadees came within whispering distance, and a blue jay squawked, irritated by something. Maybe me. Or maybe the warning of winter in its bones. At times the bursts of wind carried away the hunt's focus while delivering the sounds of the countryside putting to rest this late autumn day.

A cow bellowed at the farm in the valley, perhaps at feeding time, just before milking time. A dog's bark carried across the field. A car slowed at a driveway, and the dog barked with more gusto. And then there was quiet as the car door slammed and, I was sure, a dog's tail wagged.

Children's laughter and shouts rippled across the picked cornfield to my stand at the confluence of field and forest. The voices fell mute, and I imagined supper was ready. From another field I heard a tractor revving and clanking to load a round bale of hay before groaning out of hearing range.

Darkness gathered rapidly. I climbed down from my stand. I had heard the countryside preparing for the night, and I had heard the whistling and hissing of winter in the wind. The sound would only get louder from here on, with the days passing rapidly as I'm hurtled toward Thanksgiving, a new month, the magic and memories the first snow brings, holiday music and gift shopping, and the winter solstice.

I'll search for a Christmas tree in the woodlot. Or a honey tree at Christmas, for it was such a tree on a December day that nudged me toward the wonder of nature. It's a childhood memory in which I see my father and myself on the hillside pasture beyond our barn.

It's the afternoon of Christmas Eve. A chainsaw churns into an old oak tree. It falls to the ground. My dad stops the chainsaw, reaches into the hollow trunk and takes out pieces of honey bee combs. In the cold, the honey is too thick to drip. He places the golden combs in a stainless steel milk pail.

I recall the fascination and magic of honeycombs, of small snowflakes dancing through the gray afternoon, my cold fingers, my inquisitive dad. Did we stumble upon the bees' summer work or did dad know this present was in this tree? I think the latter, for why else would he bring along the clean pail? I'll never know for sure. Oh, the things we wish we had asked our parents.

I would guess he saw it and took note during deer hunting, or a late summer search for a cow and its newborn.

I do the same now, noting and returning to the nests of bald-faced hornets and goldfinches, and the drying stands of pearly everlasting.

I remember the afternoon growing dim as we made our way home, Christmas lights twinkling in the windows, mom's Christmas Eve meal in the oven, our sweet find in the pail. It was December, and now it is again. And now, like then, I bring home the gifts of early winter as I was taught, and the knowledge that seasons come and go, as do our trials and tribulations, as I have learned.

We find beauty and hope in the new season, the new day, the new chapter, the sweet treat in the tree

16

Walking the Land

I'd like to think the land remembers my face, my gait, and that I was a friend. Still am. Why else would I keep returning to these woods, pastures, and fields?

I come here now because I was here as a youth. Growing up here, the land etched in me the tranquility of tall pine trees, amber sunsets beyond fields of green corn, flaming maples, and fox tracks crossing fields of snow.

I nurtured a love for the land and for walking the land. There remains within me a desire to walk out the back door, through the barnyard to the pasture, up the hill and through the woods, across the town road and through the neighbors' fields, pastures and woods as I once did.

Though properties were defined by fences and roads, they remained joined by the land's flow of hills and valleys and tree lines. And the sweat of settlers.

The land I walked for miles in all directions had different owners, but owners who were not much different from each other. They were farmers bonded to their neighbors by the need for green pastures, healthy crops and livestock, and firewood. Come hunting time there was a sharing of the land to an extent I'll never see again.

These descendants of immigrant settlers from only a generation or two ago were willing to share. They lived the saying of Native Americans, "Who are we without the corn, the rabbit, the sun, the rain and the deer? Know this, my people, the all does not belong to us. We belong to the all."

When I visited this land on a mild, sunny afternoon in early November, I knew I could cross the property of at least one family, for they are the children and grandchildren of my parents' neighbors a generation ago. From our woodlot, I headed for the huge rock on the farm we once owned. The rock is in a valley of the pasture, near a small creek at the foot of tall pines. The rock is larger than a chest freezer. It begs one to pause.

I sat on the rock as a kid while exploring and later as a young man while hunting. In his journal "In Context," Native American Kenneth Cooper (Cha-das-ska-dum) wrote that the Lummi tribal members in Washington tell their children, "You sit on this rock, and I'll come back in a couple of hours, and you tell me what you learned."

Patience is what children will learn on the rock, and what we all should learn if we take the time to sit under a canopy of tranquility. I sat on the rock for a time and then pushed on to the first deer stand my dad built. The boards were rotting and crumbling. I thought I should rip the deer stand down someday. I think I don't want to.

I walked past a rock pile, covered with rolls of rusted barbed wire, where I saw a weasel for the first time. I crossed the road to the property of an absentee owner who bought the land from a family that had farmed it for generations. The new owner, who has never lived there, had the tract logged; the tall pines are gone.

I sat down on a stump and saw how the clear-cut area is filling in with saplings where pine needles once muted the footsteps of a young deer hunter. My childhood dog was a squirrel hunter, and he and I would come here on weekends to pursue the big fox squirrels in the pines and maples bordering the cornfield.

On this mild afternoon I nestled my back against the trunk of a large maple tree and slid to the ground, letting the sun find my face. I listened to a dog barking in the distance. It could have been my dog decades ago, barking at a treed squirrel from the base of this very tree.

Sunshine was melting a light cover of new snow. It felt good to sit and rest in that sun of late autumn. I don't remember tiring as a youngster. In his book *Whitetail*, George Mattis wrote about young hunters with a "love and capacity for endless walking" as they pursued deer with flush after flush over many miles.

I got up and began pushing over a series of hardwood hills, the hills I once traversed and hunted with endless enthusiasm. I crossed the tracks of deer and wild turkeys. I stood in a clearing between woodlots where I once, as a young photographer, was consumed with the golden leaves of birches against an autumnal blue sky. The birches are still there.

I turned to leave, retraced my steps to the road and caught the attention of the grandson of our neighbor from years ago. Recognizing me, he said it was not a problem that I was here; I'm welcome on his land, the land of his grandparents.

I felt warm and satisfied as I moved on, knowing at least on this day I can still walk the land of my younger days. I returned to our woods where my truck was loaded with firewood. I had remembered the land, and I felt the land remembered me.

—Journals in November—

Clouds So Swift

The clouds couldn't agree on what color to wear or their floating altitude, so they went their separate ways. Sort of. They were still loosely connected by drafts, breezes and shifting wavelengths.

The clouds wore varying soft hues, backlit by November's setting sun. There were clouds in cream to deep blue, some in shades of pink, yellow and gold. Amber, mulberry and mauve were also in the mix, and so were rose and olive. Gray clouds soared higher—a curtain pulled up to reveal the show below.

These weren't the billowing, puffy clouds against the blue sky of a summer's afternoon. They also weren't the clouds I once looked down on in amazement from a jet plane, those clouds an endless expanse of ghostly pillows illuminated by a full moon.

No, these clouds had little body, like tie-dyed shirts softly swaying toward or away from each other. The horizon, however, was jagged, with leafless treetops and bare branches poking into the swirl of color. Crows added the dimensions of motion and contrast.

Clouds swapped colors and partners as the sun, though beyond my sight, was slithering further below the horizon. Then the sun gave up on this November day. I watched the clouds blend into grayness, until the corn stubble faded into the neighboring alfalfa field, until the gathering darkness absorbed the treetops.

I walked through the field. There was silence as dusk put away its colors, except for a whisper in the cool air. A whisper saying good night.

Moonlit Dreams

A moonbeam found passage through the pines and squeezed past the highbush cranberry bush to ply its light on my pillow. I did not pull the shade. I prefer total darkness for sleep, but an exception is the light of the moon.

This beam from November's Full Beaver Moon, or Full Freezing Over Moon of the Ojibwe, has traveled 225,000 miles to cast a diffused bluish hue on my bed. I looked outside and saw the forms of trees I know so well by day. The moon had lit them, too, taking the blackness and much of the cover for mischief out of the night. No eeriness here.

When I turned off the reading lamp next to the bed the fluorescent tubes glowed in the dark. Then the subtle transformation took place. As the lamp's residue light dimmed the room actually became brighter.

Moonlight was taking over where artificial light had rather harshly glared. At the same time, my pupils were expanding, a wonderful adaptation on a night so softly lit. Soon the outline of the window was distinguishable, along with the dresser and night stand.

Looking out the window I could see the deck and make out the wind chimes seemingly suspended in air. Beyond was the mountain ash tree, its bare branches a labyrinth of jagged lines. I imagined tomorrow's daylight and the late-migrating birds that would feed on the tree's burnt orange berries.

The moon shifted, and the highbush cranberry branches fractured the moonlight coming through half of the window. Wherever and whenever there was an opening, a moonbeam took the path to my room, filling my night with satiny light and shadows.

I was being followed by a moonshadow. In the song of the same name, Cat Stevens asked of his "faithful light" the moon, "Did it take long to find me? And are you gonna stay the night?"

It had found me, that white sphere in the sky. Moonlight for a dreamy night.

Within the Hunt

This is about deer hunting but not about points and pounds. It's about a fisher and a three-toed woodpecker, nuthatches and chickadees, and bittersweet berries.

I'll walk through a dark field on opening morning of the deer hunt, wondering what it will be this season that finds me as I try to find deer. What will it be that awes me, simply because I have absorbed myself with some stealth in nature's world?

It's the hunt within the hunt, what happens during all those hours when deer aren't moving past, when rifles aren't raised. It's the little things that one looks forward to and remembers as much as the buck that falls. As the hunter grows older, it's those small portals to the natural world that keep pulling the hunter back to the woods, long after has passed the thrill of the kill.

A three-toed woodpecker was well out of its range when it came within my range during a deer hunt. The bird came flittingly close and paid me little mind for quite some time, giving me ample opportunity to study its markings. There were the distinguishing yellow crown and blurring of black and white down its back. I had never seen one, and have not seen one since.

I was sitting against the base of a large maple tree a few seasons back when the leaves began rattling behind me. Louder and louder, closer and closer. A deer? No, a deer would not be moving that fast and steady through the blowdown at my back. The noise rode a rush to my side and stopped. I looked down to see a fisher's nose inches from my right elbow. Our eyes met, eyes filled with fright. The fisher whirled and was gone. I was trembling.

In my tree stand I've had a nuthatch walk down the side of the trunk, then come around to meet me face to face. Squirrels too. A chickadee landed on my arrow once, and another time on the barrel of my rifle, on which it pecked— once—sending a metal ping through the cold air, with the chickadee in tow.

I watched a fox lope across a long field, slip into the woods and then pause directly beneath me, never knowing I was there. Another time, in a brushy swale, I walked up to a large "rock" with a sheen of charcoal. But the rock had a head, and it slowly turned to watch my approach. It was a bear, lethargic on the cusp of hibernation. I stepped away and was on my way.

There have been other, less heart-pounding close-ups, with pheasants, a barred owl, a coyote, and four ruffed grouse in a blowdown only a few feet away. While in a tree stand, a pileated woodpecker  winged past, its undulating flight path within arm's reach. I was petrified with awe.

When I walk through that field on opening morning, Orion the Hunter will guide me in my westerly course. In a hint of light over my shoulder, the eastern horizon's palette will load the hues of the dawning. Throughout the day, in stalking walks along fence lines, I will look for the orange fruit of bittersweet vine. I will bring home bittersweet if not a deer. And that will be just fine.

17

Woodland Settles into Winter

Winter settles deep into the woodland, the chilly silence pierced only by the roar of my chainsaw spinning toward the core of the hardwoods.

The saw settles into a downed oak branch, scattering wood chips on the snow while slicing off 16-inch hunks of firewood. I pick up the pieces and bang the smaller ones together. A sharp smack rings through the leafless forest.

Then the saw unsettles winter in the middle of the firm but dying tree trunk. Caramel-colored rings tell me the oak has seen many winters. This is its last.

From the still coldness to a dancing stove fire, from hanging heavy in my arms to a handful of ashes, the wood will make a journey of transformation. And it will then be gone, while a sapling faces winter, decades away from replacing the tree that nature felled for me.

I come to the woods for more than wood. In early December, I come to make sure that some deer remain after the hunt, and that the first frigid blast hasn't scared away the squirrels, rabbits, foxes and ruffed grouse. I know the answers before I arrive, but reassurance is good for the soul, and a good reason to take to the woods.

Having put the chainsaw aside, I walk the woodlot with a shotgun but without the pressure of the hunt. There is barely enough snow to cover the leaves, as the wild turkeys already know by their scratching for acorns beneath the oaks.

The turkeys have become nature's winter success story in these farm woodlots, once thought to be too far north, too cold and too much snow for the birds to survive. But here they are, winter after winter, apparently more equipped for winter's ways than we ever imagined. So am I, if I get over the first push of winter. I get back in the new season's groove with this quiet day in the woods. I'm soon as relaxed and comfortable as on a summer's day if I stay on the move and keep my back to the wind.

In her 1942 book *We Took To The Woods*, Louise Dickinson Rich writes of winter, "You can neither remodel nor ignore a thing as big as winter. In the woods we don't try. We just let winter be winter, and any adjustments that have to be made, we make in ourselves and our way of living."

I keep thinking about the words, "just let winter be winter," as I move on. I walk past a maple tree twisted to the ground by a fierce summer thunderstorm. It was a maple, its twin trunks about 12 feet up, just the right height for me to nail a small platform for a deer stand that served me well for years; the tree bordered a deer trail.

The wind that ripped apart my choice deer stand also toppled the oak and white ash trees I cut up for firewood. Nature gives and takes. I discover another downed white ash. Leaves remain on its branches, above where rabbit tracks have flattened the snow on trips to some dark, safe spot beneath the blowdown. I survey the scene and know I can cut up most of the tree without disturbing the rabbit's winter hideout.

There are squirrel tracks and digs for acorns in the snow. I follow grouse tracks until they go in a circle. I walk in a circle before stopping, somewhat perplexed, a bit embarrassed. Then I realize the bird has wings. I don't. I give up the track.

As the afternoon wanes the half-lit first quarter moon starts to brighten quite high in the eastern sky. The full moon is exactly a week away, when the large sphere will rise at sunset. It's a dreamy afternoon, and I think of the song verse, "There's a new moon on the fourteenth, first quarter twenty-first, and a full moon in the last week brings a fullness to the earth."

I feel the fullness. It's getting dark fast as I haul my firewood to the truck. I pick up the pace and start sweating despite the chill that rides in on the sunset. I drive away, content that nature here is well, making all the adjustments for another winter.

—Journals in December—

Smoke Ghosts

There were white ghosts and black ghosts, dancing away in the fading glow of the full moon an hour before sunrise. The ghosts were racing for cover in the dim of dawn.

Was it their past the ghosts sought after they took a harrowing heated escape up the chimney on this bone-chilling morning? But the ghosts had no bones. They leaped from the chimney with dizzying fluidity, whirling and swirling, rising and falling and rising again as if eluding invisible obstacles in their break for freedom.

They were wood stove ghosts. I wondered if their release from the hot coals sent them looking for the forest where they once lived in maple, oak and ash trees. Would they spend the rest of their days hidden high in the branches, wisps of the past witnessing secrets of the present?

I stared at a snow-covered backyard dimly lit by the Full Cold Moon, now high in the west behind me and casting shadows from all the familiar characters—the birdhouse, the trellis, the deck posts. The smoke ghosts were not as serene and steady. They were white against the cold predawn sky as they flowed in waves from the chimney. But on the snow below, their flickering shadows were dark.

The ghosts were hard to follow, their forms changing with the whims of any slight breeze. I watched some race through the herb garden, bounce off the yard shed, climb the shed's roof and disappear in the branches beyond. They were free, no longer standing in the forest, stacked in a pile or trapped in a stove. Now the ghosts danced in the branches. A cold winter waltz.

Trail of the Cat

I was on top of the cat before I knew it. Before the cat knew it too, or so I thought.

My cross-country skis had sped me down a short, steep hill. The trail curved into the meadow. Cattails blurred past. Then suddenly there was the real cat tail on an orange body, right in the middle of the trail, a mile from the nearest farm.

I snowplowed to a stop a few feet from the cat. It looked young, a kitten, and frail. I was amused that it was facing the other way and didn't hear or see me approach.

"Hello kitty," I said. No reaction. It never moved. I studied the cat from behind. I paused a long minute, wondering why the cat wasn't moving. Then it slowly lifted a paw and put it back down in the snow. And then again. It seemed to not have the strength or will to walk.

I slid closer. The cat was oblivious to my presence. I finally reached my gloved hand down to touch it, hoping there wouldn't be a frightened reaction. The cat barely responded to my touch.

As I stepped back to assess the situation the cat let out a mournful cry that pierced the silence of the late afternoon chill trapped beneath the steely sky. I knew it was a cry for help. I had no choice, knowing the cat would not live through this winter's night.

I figured I could ski with one pole, so if the cat wasn't scared and wiggly, I could carry it to my truck. I lifted the thin, seemingly weightless orange bundle of fur and cradled it against my chest. It did not protest. I turned around and began to ski-step up the hill.

It became apparent to me the cat was blind. The little tabby crawled on my shoulder and then, amazingly, stretched its body across the back of my shoulders. I skied a bit hunch-backed for the mile to my truck. I knew I had the kitten's total trust when it began purring in my ear. It couldn't see, but it sure could feel my good intentions.

When I got the cat home I fed it and cleaned it up. We warmed up to each other, figuratively and literally. But being in no position to care for a cat beyond this emergency, I called the animal shelter. I checked a week later and was told the cat was adopted by a little girl who immediately fell in love with it and had no qualms about caring for a blind kitty.

From a cold swamp to a child's warm love and adoration, the kitten had made the journey. Part of it by skis.

Winter Solstice

Winter arrives on the calendar this week. So what should I expect from winter? The worst, I suppose, if I so choose to look at it that way.

But what if I expect the best of winter, of the gems to come, found in the serenity of snow and cold? These gems will surely turn my head even as I turn my collar to the wind.

It's already happening. I see the wide flowerheads of faded, bronzed sedum dressed up in white hats. Chimney smoke curls into the frigid night air, softly illuminated by holiday lights as the wisps tease the crescent moon.

There's more to come. I'll see swirls and whirls of frost on the window panes of an old shed. An icicle will hang in the bushes, changing colors as it catches the sunset's golden rays. The same rays will find their way through a south window, warming a nook for reading a book.

I'll study tracks in the snow, discovering the night moves of a rabbit to and from the seeds below the bird feeder. I'll see deer tracks sharing my snowshoe path. A cardinal will appear among the first fat snowflakes of an approaching storm, flashing its red feathers as a warning to all birds to feed and take shelter.

Winter is bright red high-bush cranberries against a backdrop of pine boughs laden with snowy fingers, dogs bouncing in the fluffy whiteness with hints of fun of their noses, lake ice booming in the darkness, the lonesome hoots of an owl at midnight, and geese shrouded in the rising steam as river water meets a morning of zero degrees.

Perhaps I'll approach a feeding chickadee, so close I can feel the energy of its dime-weight body vibrating for warmth. Yes, warmth, what we all seek now. I'll carry an armful of warmth from the wood pile for the late afternoon's repose, the serenity slipping into a cozy evening. Then, a quiet morning indoors, warmed by the wood heat and hot coffee.

It's winter. Sometimes the best of times.

18

Trailing to A New Year

I went for a snowshoe jog today as the old year was winding down. I knew well the trail I chose, where it meanders through a meadow begging for exploration, where the going is easy across a field on the way to the woods, where a hill makes me work, where the wind may find me, where the tall pines move me to stop and gaze. And there is always a surprise, if only a cottontail flashing across the trail.

What should I feel as something anew, as big as a new year, is stirring on this New Year's Eve? What fresh emotions and inspiring notions might come over me as tomorrow's sunrise yawns over the horizon?

I know the new year will bring the same seasons. But will the scenes and actors change? Will the new year afford new opportunities to surprise a coyote in the winter whiteness, discover a fox den of kits in spring, catch brook trout in the soft summer rain, or stumble across a secluded apple tree in fall?

I see the new year as a trail laid out in front of me, but I know not where it will take me. I only know it begins and ends with winter on either side of spring, summer and fall. Will there be explorations and pleasing vistas? Will there be easy stretches? Will I have to run against the wind at times? Where will the hills come? How steep?

What about surprises and setbacks? Am I prepared? Will I be happy tracing the new trail?

I have no resolutions, but wonder if I will be resolute. If the birds and animals are my guide, then I will be resolute to not rush time, only follow time while allowing it to carry me from season to season, solstice to solstice, equinox to equinox. One day at a time.

I often exist in fits of hurry, the only order in the day that of what needs attention next on my list. Has the day produced? What did I accomplish? Nature, however, pays calm, instinctive attention to the daily small stuff. The birds and critters, and trees and rivers, paint the big picture slowly and steadily on the canvas of each year. I should too.

For now, my new year begins with finding Orion and Sirius in the midnight sky. Tomorrow I'll watch for the first fat snowflakes of an afternoon snowfall. And after that snowfall, at nightfall, with the air so fresh and the snow pristine, I'll go for a walk, embracing the new year all around me.

Acknowledgments

This book has been at least 20 years in the making, considering that parts of it originated from my newspaper columns and essays appearing in the *Rice Lake Chronotype* (WI). Though much of the book was written after retiring from the *Chronotype*, some of the pieces first appeared in the newspaper and have been rewritten, for content and length, for *Soul of the Outdoors*. I am grateful for permission from *Chronotype* owner Adams Publishing Group to use those works, and also from the *Chronotype*'s former owners, the Dorrance family.

I want to thank friends and colleagues for their encouragement and honest criticism, and for initial proofreading. That proofreading began with Sharon Schaefer at the newspaper, and, in the early stages of the manuscript, Leiah Fundell, Troy Espe, Gene Prigge, and my wife, Cathy.

Other colleagues and authors helped me with their insight and reviews, including Patti See, Joe Knight, Timothy Goodwin, BJ Hollars, Peter Davidson, and Dan Lyksett. I also want to acknowledge all the instructors who were instrumental in my pursuit of writing, including my high school newspaper advisor Joe Gasperini, and my college journalism advisor Leslie Polk. I am forever indebted to the late Warren Leary, the *Chronotype* publisher who hired me straight out of college. He was both my toughest critic and biggest fan.

Finally, the book would not have become a reality without Dr. Ross Tangedal, publisher and director at Cornerstone Press, UW-Stevens Point. Dr. Tangedal saw the merits in my manuscript, and he and his staff, including Ava Willet, Sophie McPherson, and Natalie Reiter, worked closely with me. A special thanks goes to Cornerstone Press editorial director Ellie Atkinson for her attention to detail and open dialogue during several rounds of editing. The Cornerstone staff was receptive to my many tweaking requests, cover to cover, to see *Soul of the Outdoors* through to publication.

DAVE GRESCHNER is an award-winning outdoor writer and columnist. He served as the sports/outdoors editor at the *Rice Lake Chronotype* in northwest Wisconsin for over forty years, where he won twenty Wisconsin Newspaper Association first-place awards. *Soul of the Outdoors* is his first book.

www.ingramcontent.com/pod-product-compliance
Lightning Source LLC
Chambersburg PA
CBHW031414120626
46545CB00006B/2131